ME AND THE ORGONE

ORSON BEAN

ME
and the
ORGONE

Introduction by A. S. Neill

ST. MARTIN'S PRESS   NEW YORK

AFFILIATED PUBLISHERS: Macmillan & Company, Limited,
London—also at Bombay, Calcutta, Madras and Melbourne—
The Macmillan Company of Canada, Limited, Toronto.

FOR CAROLYN

FOREWORD

This book is about Orson Bean's experience with Reichian
therapy and how he set up his school on 15th Street in
New York City. I take the latter first. I saw it, and even
though tired after crossing the ocean, and chary of climb-
ing the stairs in his school, I saw a few of the pupils. To
me, the criterion of a school is the eyes of the kids. I condemn all state institutions that treat problem children with
the methods that made them problems—fear, discipline,
punishment. The eyes of such children frighten one. The
eyes of the 15th Street pupils showed—pro-lifeness is
probably the best word.

Orson's description of his orgone therapy with Elsworth

Baker makes exciting reading. How it will be taken by folks who never heard of Reich I cannot guess; to me it brought back memories of when I lay naked on a couch and old Reich made me squirm when he attacked my stiff muscles. Luckily one does not recall pain; I doubt if one can recall pleasure. Orson's descriptions are valuable mainly for this reason—that so far books about the method have been written by practitioners, not by patients, e.g. Baker's *Man In The Trap*.

Orson had an experience similar to my own. I had more emotional reaction after six weeks on Reich's couch than I had after years in "talking" analysis. It was later that I came across Reich's criticism of psychoanalysis, that it deals with words, while all the damage is done to the child before it can talk. A profound criticism, which cannot apply to the release of muscle tension, another pre-speech affair.

It is embarrassing to write about friends. Orson and Carolyn charmed me when I met them in New York. I had expected to meet a typical TV personality . . . self-centered, superficial, brash. It was a delightful shock to find that Orson was just a guy, a human guy. So many screen people are shells of outward correctness, armored, not only as we all are by our training, but armored against betraying a real personality in front of the camera. Orson escaped all that. His book makes no attempt to create a popular image. He bares his soul, shows us a man who has no need to pretend. I hesitate to claim that his therapy with Baker did the trick because without therapy others have been sincere in their lives. . . . Einstein, Gandhi, Lincoln, and of course Jesus. Yet it is obvious that therapy

vii

helped Orson a lot. Myself I think that analysis made me see the other fellow's point of view, so that I find it difficult to condemn. Maybe all types of therapy make one tolerant. Reich's sure does, although Reich wasn't very tolerant himself . . . *vide* Ilse Reich's *Life*. His intolerance was one against what he called the emotional plague, a real thing but apt to be misapplied too often. When I once made a criticism of Reich one of his trained doctors pointed a finger at me.

"Emotional plague, Neill," he said sternly.

This book will be met with the scorn and hate of so many Reich enemies who dismiss him as a madman. I cannot judge. He was sane when I met him for the last time in 1948. If his mind became unbalanced later it would not surprise me. Often he said that our asylums are full of people who aren't mad enough to live in our sick civilization. But what if he did go mad? Many great men have lost their reason. . . . Nietzsche, Swift, Ruskin, Schumann. I know I am no genius for I haven't gone mad, and if at last I become a senile raving man of 90 that fact will not alter the fact that I founded Summerhill. Anyway it is an odd world if Reich were mad and the politicians and the Pentagon and the color-haters are sane.

Reich was a great man and I have often been thankful that I had the good fortune to meet him, to love him, and to be loved by him. Orson never knew him, but he has grasped what Reich's message to humanity means.

A. S. Neill
Summerhill

ONE

I was living, in those days, in an apartment in New York City that looked out onto the East River. My marriage of six years had busted up and my ex-wife had gone to live in, of all places, Africa, where she had a new French husband and a new life. For my part, I had a year-and-a-half-old baby daughter, Michele, and a beautiful seventeen-year-old Irish nanny to look after her. Her name was Bridie and my wife had hired her as a maid and I had kept her on to look after the baby when my wife departed. She had a rosy-cheeked, peasanty, droit-du-seigneur beauty and a body that made Raquel Welch look like a rake. It was an odd situation: a horny, miserable bachelor, a year-and-a-half-old baby girl and this ravishing Irish teen-ager occupying a luxury flat on Manhattan's East Side.

Bridie was a darling and the two of us would take little Michele for walks in Carl Schurz Park up by Gracie Mansion near our apartment building. I would affection-

1

ately put my arm around her shoulder or waist as we walked along or we would each hold one of Michele's hands and swing her between us. The tight-faced wives of advertising executives sitting on benches watching their offspring climb in and out of the sandboxes would look up as we walked past and out of the corner of my eye I could see them discussing us. Madison Avenue acquaintances of mine would tell me that they had heard I had a real swinging scene going on up on East End Avenue. It was news to me—I never laid a glove on Bridie. Not that I didn't want to, mind you, but I restrained myself, remembering Goethe's classic admonition: "Don't muck up a good thing!"

I went through a year of dark gloom, feeling sorry for myself. Every morning I would drink my breakfast coffee by the big picture window that looked out on the river and contemplate the scuz, orange peels and Old Nick wrappers that floated by. There was really something therapeutic about watching the flow of the water, which is why I had gone about finding an apartment on the river when my marriage broke up. I emerged out of my dark year and began haunting Dick Edwards' bar on East Sixty-first Street each night, looking for love. I got myself a job in a play called *Never Too Late,* which turned out to be a hit, and one night a friend of mine came to see it and we went out for a drink afterwards. "Did you know," he said, "that there is a new form of psychiatry that says that if you can have a good come, all your neuroses will go away?" My friend never wastes words.

I told him that I knew nothing about it, but that it

2

sounded intriguing. I asked him if there were a book on the subject.

"I'll bring you one," he said.

I went home to my apartment that night and sat looking out at the river, thinking.

Eleven years earlier I had gone into psychoanalysis. I hadn't felt suicidal at the age of twenty-four or even actively miserable. I had simply felt a nagging void in my solar plexus that continuously mumbled, "There must be more to life than this." I had found myself an excellent Freudian psychiatrist and worked with him for ten years. I had learned a lot about myself, spent twenty-five thousand dollars, gotten married and divorced and at the end of the ten years the void in my solar plexus was still mumbling. I'm not saying that I didn't benefit from the experience; I wasn't unhappy in the same way I had been ten years before. But I was unhappy. I was also ten years older and twenty-five thousand dollars poorer. And I was befuddled. I had, in the course of my analysis, seen friends of mine who were obviously copping out: dropping in and out of analysis, changing doctors, wasting time, lying to the analyst and, in general, not coming to grips with the world. I, on the other hand, had picked a good, tough man and stuck with him for ten long years, doggedly pursuing self-knowledge and growth, and it hadn't worked. On the last session of my psychoanalysis, the good doctor and I had shaken hands. He had told me that it had been a pleasure to work with me and I had thanked him and he had assured me that I could come and see him whenever I had a problem to discuss. I had walked out of his office thinking, "When is it going to happen? When do I feel like an analyzed person? When do I stop being anxious and apprehensive?" I figured that maybe it took a while for it all to sink in and I should just go about my business and gradually the magic change would occur. It hadn't.

I sat, that night, by the window and thought about what my friend had said . . . "a new form of psychiatry that says if you can have a good come, all your neuroses will go away." God, what a simple thought, but what a true one. Thinking back over my life, I realized that with all my various and sundry sexual activities, most of my comes, to put it bluntly, had been lousy. The handful (pardon the expression) of times that I had had a really good come I had felt wonderful for the next few days. Not just wonderful, but liberated . . . liberated from thoughts of sex, for one thing, which made me realize that the reason for my constant preoccupation with it was probably that it was continuously disappointing. It seemed to me, as I thought back to those few and far between great comes of mine, that in the days that followed them I had felt an incredible energy and zest for living; indeed it had actually seemed that I was happy. That night I felt like Saul on the road to Damascus. I had seen a blinding light and happiness was within my grasp.

Then my friend dropped the book off at my theater—*The Function of the Orgasm* by Wilhelm Reich. "Oh Christ," I thought, "this is nothing new. It's that nut with the orgone box." I vaguely knew about Reich, having heard dribs and drabs of opinions about him over the years. He had been a great psychiatrist back in the days of Freud and Vienna. His book *Character Analysis* is considered a classic and is still must reading for young psychiatrists. But after *Character Analysis* it was said that he had gone off the deep end. He had sex on the brain and his orgone box was something that people would sit in naked. It wasn't powered by anything but it was supposed to have collected rays of some sort that either made you feel sexy or cured cancer or something. He had come to America and the government had arrested him as a quack and he had died in prison. They say he used to masturbate his patients or have them engage in supposedly therapeutic orgies. He was some kind of a communist and there's still a small cult of people who insist that he wasn't crazy but that he was a great man.

I was bitterly disappointed. Still, the title was intriguing so I began to read the book. It was like trying to get through the Torah. I had to go back and reread every paragraph but as I plowed on I found, to my amazement, that the nut was making sense. I spent my days studying the book and I carried it to the theater with me every night. One of my costars in the play was Maureen O'Sullivan and I would sit in her dressing room and read passages to her. I became consumed with Reich and his ideas and sought out other books by and about him. He had been born in Austria in 1897 and studied medicine and psychiatry with Freud. He had become a member of Freud's inner circle, but he could never accept the idea that for a patient to lie on a couch and simply talk was a meaningful form of treatment for emotional problems. More and more, he became convinced that sexual frustration was at the bottom of every disturbance. Freud and his fol-

5

lowers believed that sexual difficulties were much more widespread among women than among men. Reich disagreed with this and felt that men and women were equally troubled and that the trouble was nearly universal. He also disagreed with Freud's concept of "voluntary renunciation." Reason told him that if repressing sexual drives caused emotional disturbances, then, voluntary renunciation of them was not going to help much. What he called his "thin red line of logic" carried him out of the field of psychiatry and into other sciences. After many years of work, he arrived at what he called the orgasm theory. It was this orgasm theory which brought the wrath of organized psychiatry down on his head and drove him in disgrace from the socially accepted world of medicine. It was the same orgasm theory which now held me absolutely spellbound.

TWO

Night after night at the theater and day after day in my apartment on the East River, I read Reich's *Function of the Orgasm.*

It took me a long time to understand, even intellectually, the orgasm theory but I finally did and here, in over-simplified, but basically accurate form, is what it is: Human beings, like all living things from the amoeba on up have within them an energy, hithertofore undetected. Reich discovered it and called it orgone energy (from the root of the word organism). This energy is, in effect, the life force, not in any mystical sense, but physically. The energy is built up by intake of food, fluid and air and is also absorbed directly through the skin.

Orgone energy streams rhythmically and continuously through the body from the top of the head to the bottom of the feet and back again and in the ideally healthy and natural person, it can be felt as a pleasurable, glowing sensation of health and well-being. It is discharged by activity, excretion, emotional expression, the process of thinking and by conversion into body heat, which radiates to the environment. It is also used up in growth. In the normal course of things, more energy is built up than is discharged. This extra energy is stored for emergency situations such as battle or exhausting work. But when no emergency exists, the energy keeps piling up so that the organism would have to grow continuously or would eventually burst unless there were some mechanism to discharge the accumulated excess energy after it had reached a certain level. In healthy individuals, this level is felt as sexual excitation. The build-up of energy creates a tension and the method that nature has created for relieving this tension and regulating the build-up is the sexual orgasm. The deep feeling of relaxation which follows a truly satisfying sexual climax is indicative of this release from tension. But the tension is relieved and the energy regulated only when the individual is capable of full, healthy, loving, sexual fulfillment. An unrewarding or compulsive sexual experience doesn't work. The orgasm must be deeply pleasurable and it must be followed spontaneously by complete relaxation or the orgone energy has not been discharged. This lack of discharge is felt as tension or restlessness. In the healthy individual, the need for sexual surrender and release is based entirely on this ebb and flow of orgone energy.

For untold centuries, man, alone among the other animals, has interfered with his own natural functioning by preventing the flow, build-up and release of his orgone energy. He has done this by making himself incapable of full, natural, healthy, sexual gratification through a process that Reich calls armoring. Here is what armoring is: Certain muscles of the body help to control the emotions. For instance, when a child sobs, his whole body shakes uncontrollably. His lower lip quivers, his chest expands and contracts, his solar plexus heaves and his tear ducts produce tears. Over the years of their childhood, most children learn that sobbing is socially unacceptable, to one degree or another. A child ordered to "stop that crying" has no choice but to do so, and the way he does it is by clamping down on the controlling muscles; the solar plexus is tightened, the lower lip is stiffened and the muscles around the eyes are held back. The crying stops and the child is then rewarded by being told that he is "a little man" or "a good girl" and social approval cinches the deal. In time the armoring becomes chronic and the child becomes unable to sob.

Rage is equally unacceptable in society. Watch a young child having a tantrum. This is the natural human physical expression of rage: kicking, yelling at the top of one's lungs, beating with the fists. Many muscles come into play in the course of the free expression of rage. When a child is continually frustrated and made furious but prevented from expressing the fury, he has no choice but to suppress it. This is done, in the beginning, not on an intellectual level, but by deadening the feeling in the muscles involved in kicking, beating, screaming, biting or whatever the child feels the need to do.

Pleasurable sensations in the genital area are perceived to be dangerous by the child in our society. Even the child in an "enlightened" home gets the message after a while when he finds himself distracted every time his hands get close to the danger zone. Deadening the feeling in the entire area is safer than continuing to experience the natural pleasant sensations and being tempted to heighten them by manipulation.

One deadens feeling by tightening muscles. Over the years, this tightening and deadening becomes chronic until the musculature of one's own body becomes a veritable armor against unacceptable feelings. Reich found that the muscles which tend to get armored are the ones that go crosswise in the body, across the eyes, mouth, chest, solar plexus, pelvis, etc. As they become chronically hardened, they interfere with the pleasurable, up and down, head-to-toe streamings of the orgone energy. (It's interesting that in all cultures "yes" is expressed by shaking the head up and down, "no" by shaking the head crosswise, side to side.) When the orgone energy cannot stream and build-up in its natural fashion, sexual self-regulation ceases to operate.

In the healthy, unarmored, self-regulated person, the whole process of sex is quite different from the way it is with an armored person. In the healthy person, the sex drive is not separated from love but is, rather, the physical counterpart of it. The truly self-regulated person never uses sex for self-aggrandizement or power or control or subjugation. Rather, he feels it as an overpowering need to melt into another, to become physically one with his love object. He is filled with tenderness and caring and concern for his partner at the height of the sex act. The world falls away and indeed they do become one for the moment, for at orgasm, true orgasm, the energy fields of the partners fuse and merge as the excess energy is released through the genitals. Any idea of using, or humiliating, or degrading or "screwing" the partner is

10

alien and unthinkable, and afterwards the feeling is one of love and tenderness and deep gratitude.

In neurotic, armored people, sexual strivings are felt through deadened and hardened muscles. The soft, warm, tender glow felt by the self-regulated person is absent and in its place is a desperate feeling of wanting to "break out" of one's own body. For the armored person, the sex act seems to be filled with danger. All the old childish anxieties come up with the sexual excitation: the mixed feelings, the guilt, the castration fears. To "succeed" becomes the end-all of the act, to "get it up" or "lay her" or "make her come." Fantasies are employed to overcome the anxieties that make completion of the act impossible. But the fantasies make the act unreal and destroy any feeling of tenderness and finally when the desperate grinding is over there is the inevitable letdown, the feeling of self-loathing and disgust and "what's the meaning of it all?"

"If only we didn't have this disgusting sex drive in us that takes up so much of our time and energy and then lets us down," says the armored person, and in his fantasy and his literature heaven is a place with no sex.

Reich's treatment consisted, in a nutshell, of breaking down the armoring and thereby restoring the natural self-regulative process. Using his physician's knowledge of musculature, he discovered exactly which muscles controlled which functions. He found that by kneading, pressing or jabbing at certain muscles used to inhibit crying, he could make the patient spontaneously start to sob and he found that other muscles, when jabbed at or pressed, would cause rage-filled screaming. He encouraged his patients to give in to these natural functions.

11

At first, the patients felt embarrassed to rant and rave and sob but in a short time they felt overwhelming relief at being able to express their feelings fully. Reich discovered that as his patients found themselves able to cry and rage again, the old feelings from the days when they originally armored themselves came to the surface and could be analyzed. The armoring, it seemed, was not symptomatic of neurosis but was, in fact, the actual physical counterpart of the neurosis. As it was broken down, vivid dreams occurred which the patient was often spontaneously able to analyze himself. Reich found that in his armored patients breathing was shallow, and he worked with them to get them to breathe more freely and deeply. The holding in of the chest and diminishing of the breathing function was in itself, it turned out, a defense mechanism against feelings in the area. When this defense was broken down, all kinds of deep feelings flooded out, which under classical psychiatry would have taken years to reach, if they could be reached at all.

Reich discovered that it was very important for a doctor to learn in what order the armoring should be broken down (eyes and mouth first, chest second, etc.). He also learned that the very thing the patient wanted, freedom from his internal bondage, was what terrified him most. As each new area of armoring was broken down, the patient would feel elated at first and then absolutely terrified. It was as though the armoring had become part of the personality and as *it* went, he felt that *he* was going. Patients told him they literally felt they were going to die, that they were coming apart, that they had nothing to hold onto. All Reich could do was counsel them to tolerate the fear and tell themselves that they weren't going to die. Those who were able to stick it out found themselves changing profoundly.

After the armoring of the eyes, mouth, chest, etc., had been dissolved, the final area of armoring that Reich would attempt to break down was the pelvic region, which controlled the genital-anal area. Not until a patient was able to sob uncontrollably, as if his heart would break, scream with fury and kick and pound the couch until his stored-up rage was all gotten out, not until he was able to feel the deep, aching longing he had felt as a little child who had needed his mother, could Reich even approach this hottest spot of all. The terror, hatred and rage released as feeling flowed back into the deadened pelvis was fearsome, and handling it required all of Reich's skill. But the pelvis also contained man's deepest longings. Those for whom the therapy worked completely, achieved what Reich called "orgastic potency." Up until this time, it had been thought that there were two kinds of sexual potency: erectile and ejaculative. Reich found that these two were merely steps on the way to full sexual capacity or "orgastic potency." This, he found, occurs when the unarmored person is able to surrender totally with mind and body, without fantasies or reservations, to the partner and the sexual experience. When this happens, the total organism is involved, with nothing held back. It is the most transcendent experience possible in life. At the apex of the act when the union is complete and the two separate energy fields merge and become one, the partners feel a unity with the entire universe. For a person capable of achieving this, even once, the question of what life is all about never has to be asked again. It is this specific goal that Wilhelm Reich's orgone therapy attempts to achieve.

13

THREE

The architects who design theaters hate actors and the dressing rooms are always dreadful little closets. The better rooms are jealously sought after for both comfort and status. When *Never Too Late* opened at the Playhouse Theater on Forty-eighth Street in New York (since torn down to make room for the expanded Rockefeller Center), I decided to escape the rat race and I found a little suite of rooms on the fourth floor of the backstage area which no one else wanted because of the long walk up the stairs. I painted it and hung curtains and I brought in a TV set and some furniture. Maureen O'Sullivan's daughter, Mia Farrow, had come to New York from London to live with her mother for the run of the play. Mia would hang around the theater every night, since she knew no one in town, and she soon made friends with the cast. My room, with space to sit down and a TV set, became sort of a social center for the younger members of the company and Mia would be in there every night listening to my stuff about

14

orgonomy. One night she said, "Did you know that Ursula knows all about Reich?" Ursula was a young woman who worked with the show as a dresser, helping the actresses with their quick changes, etc. I walked downstairs and found Ursula and said, "What do you know about Wilhelm Reich?"

"Well, not all that much," she said, "but I have a friend named Paul Matthews who is very close to a Reichian doctor. Would you like to meet Paul?"

"Sure," I said.

Ursula made a call and the following night Matthews and I sat down over drinks at Dick Edward's bar. We talked about Fidel Castro for a while and then we started discussing Reich. Matthews asked me why I was interested and what I wanted to see a Reichian doctor for. As I answered he sat staring at me, taking in every word. I felt as though I was going through an audition. I told him about my chance introduction to Reich's writings and about my growing excitement with his ideas. I told him of my disenchantment with psychoanalysis and how everything I had read indicated that Reich's treatment methods seemed to fill in the gaps in Freudian analysis. When I had finished talking, Paul Matthews sat there and thought for a little while and then he took out a piece of paper and a pencil and wrote down the name Elsworth Baker, M.D., with an address and phone number. The address turned out to be two blocks down from me on East End Avenue across from the park where Bridie and I went for walks with Michele. I thanked him and went home very excited. The next afternoon I called Dr. Baker. Paul Matthews, it turned out, had phoned him in the morning and Baker would see me that Tuesday at 2 P.M.

15

When Tuesday came, I left my apartment early and walked leisurely through Carl Schurz Park along the river. It was a cool brisk day and here and there little steam vapors rose from the spots where a poodle had passed before being pulled along by a doorman. I picked my way carefully through the park, thanking God that people don't keep elephants in New York. I entered Dr. Baker's building, a big modern apartment house, and inquired of the man at the reception desk where his office was. He told me, and either I imagined it or he looked at me strangely. I walked down a long hall toward the door at the end. There was an unusual odor in the corridor as I approached Baker's door, a fresh smell but a heightened one, sort of like ozone. I couldn't pin it down. I tried the door and it was open, so I walked into a large room which would have been the living room if the place were being used as an apartment. There was a couch and a coffee table with up-to-date *Life* magazines on it. I could see a typically small kitchen and a bathroom and between them was a door which obviously led to a bedroom. Through the door I could hear the faint sound of a girl crying. It was about five of two. I waited, leafing through a magazine, for about ten minutes. The door to the bedroom opened and before I could look up I heard the bathroom door close. The girl had apparently darted out and run into the john. A couple minutes later Dr. Baker walked into the living room. He was a slight man with deep-set, intense eyes.

"How do you do," he said. "Won't you come in?"

I preceded him into the inner room. It had a small cot in it, covered by a freshly laundered sheet, and a desk with a chair on either side of it and another chair against

16

the wall. There were venetian blinds on the window and an amateurishly painted picture on the wall, done, I imagined, by a patient. The entire apartment was painted a milk chocolate brown and it had wall to wall carpeting in tan.

Dr. Baker sat down behind his desk and indicated the chair in front of it for me. I could faintly hear the girl crying in the bathroom behind me. He took a notebook and a pen out of his desk and asked my full name, age, address, etc. Then he leaned back in his chair and said, "Why are you interested in working with me?" I told him that I had completed a supposedly successful psycho-analysis of ten years' duration, that I had worked hard and had gone, I felt, as far as the doctor had been able to take me and that I felt basically unsatisfied with the results of it and with my life. I told him that I had a thriving career and a baby daughter whom I loved and an active sex life, although no woman whom I cared about since the departure of my wife. I said that I wasn't de-pressed or specifically unhappy but that I would never be satisfied until I felt fulfilled and, dare I say it, really happy. I told him of how I had happened to read Reich's *Function of the Orgasm* and of how I had known the principle was right the moment I had heard of it. Behind me I heard the toilet flush and the bathroom door open and then the front door open and close.

Dr. Baker said, "I see." He looked at me the way Paul Matthews had done. "Well," he said, "take off your clothes and let's have a look at you." My eyes went glassy as I stood up and started to undress—"You can leave on your shorts and socks," said Baker, to my relief. I laid my clothes on the chair against the wall in a neat pile,

17

hoping to get a gold star. "Lie down on the bed," said the doctor. "Yes, sure," said Willie the Robot, and did so. "Just breathe naturally," he said, pulling a chair over to the bed and sitting down next to me. I fixed my eyes on a spot of water damage near the upper left-hand corner of Doctor Baker's window and breathed naturally. I thought: "What if I get an erection, or shit on his bed or vomit." The doctor was feeling the muscles around my jaw and neck. He found a tight cord in my neck, pressed it hard and kept on pressing it. It hurt like hell but Little Lord Jesus no crying he makes. "Did that hurt?" asked Dr. Baker.

"Well, a little," I said, not wanting to be any trouble.

"Only a little?" he said.

"Well, it hurt a lot," I said. "It hurt like hell."

"Why didn't you cry?"

"I'm a grown-up."

He began pinching the muscles in the soft part of my shoulders. I wanted to smash him in his sadistic face, put on my clothes and get the hell out of there. Instead I said "Ow." Then I said "That hurts."

"It doesn't sound as if it hurts," he said.

"Well, it does," I said, and managed an "Ooo, Ooo."

"Now breathe in and out deeply," he said and he placed the palm of one hand on my chest and pushed down hard on it with the other. The pain was substantial. "What if the bed breaks?" I thought. "What if my spine snaps or I suffocate?"

I breathed in and out for a while and then Baker found my ribs, and began probing and pressing.

I thought of Franchot Tone in the torture scene from

18

Lives of a Bengal Lancer. I managed to let out a few pitiful cries which I hoped would break Baker's heart. He began to jab at my stomach, prodding here and there to find a tight little knotted muscle. I no longer worried about getting an erection, possibly ever, but the possibility of shitting on his bed loomed even larger. He moved downward, mercifully passing my jockey shorts, I don't know what I had expected him to do, measure my cock or something, and began to pinch and prod the muscles of my inner thighs. At that point I realized that the shoulders and the ribs and the stomach hadn't hurt at all. The pain was amazing, especially since it was an area I hadn't thought would ever hurt. Notwithstanding, my feeble vocal expressions were nothing that would have shamed Freddie Bartholomew.

"Turn over," said Baker. I did and he started at my neck and worked downwards with an unerring instinct for every tight, sore muscle. He pressed and kneaded and jabbed and if I were Franchot Tone I would have sold out the entire Thirty-first Lancers. "Turn back over again," said Dr. Baker and I did. "All right," he said, "I want you to breathe in and out as deeply as you can and at the same time roll your eyes around without moving your head. Try to look at all four walls, one at a time, and move your eyeballs as far from side to side as possible." I began to roll my eyes, feeling rather foolish but grateful that he was no longer tormenting my body. On and on my eyes rolled. "Keep breathing," said Baker. I began to feel a strange pleasurable feeling in my eyes like the sweet fuzziness that happens when you smoke a good stick of pot. The fuzziness began to spread through my face and

19

head and then down into my body. "All right," said Baker. "Now I want you to continue breathing and do a bicycle kick on the bed with your legs." I began to raise my legs and bring them down rhythmically, striking the bed with my calves. My thighs began to ache and I wondered when he would say that I had done it long enough, but he didn't. On and on I went, until my legs were ready to drop off. Then, gradually, it didn't hurt anymore and that same sweet fuzzy sensation of pleasure began to spread through my whole body, only much stronger. I now felt as if a rhythm had taken over my kicking which had nothing to do with any effort on my part. I felt transported and in the grip of something larger than me. I was breathing more deeply than I ever had before and I felt the sensation of each breath all the way down past my lungs and into my pelvis. Gradually, I felt myself lifted right out of Baker's milk chocolate room and up into the spheres. I was beating to an astral rhythm. Finally, I knew it was time to stop. I lay there for how many minutes I don't know and I heard his voice say, "How do you feel?"

"Wonderful," I said. "Is this always what happens?"

"More or less," he said. "I can see you on Tuesdays at two. Ideally I'd like to see you twice a week but I don't have the time and once a week is more than sufficient."

I stood up shakily and began to pull on my clothes. "I'm a bit dizzy," I said.

"You'll be all right," he said. "Just take it easy. Actually, you're in pretty good shape. It shouldn't take too long."

We agreed on a price per hour, I finished dressing, shook his hand and walked out into the waiting room. A bald-headed man sat there reading *Life* magazine. He didn't look up. I wondered how long he had been there and if he had heard my noises in the other room. I walked out the door and down the hall. It seemed as if my feet barely touched the carpeted halls. I came out into the air and crossed the street into the park. I looked up into the sky over the East River. It was a deeper blue than any I had seen in my life, and there seemed to be little flickering pinpoints of light in it. I looked at the trees. They were a richer green than I had ever seen. It seemed as though all my senses were heightened. I was perceiving everything with greater clarity. I walked home feeling exhilarated and bursting with energy. That night I went to work at the theater and got through the show somehow. I didn't know if I was good or bad. I got home sometime after midnight and I knew there was no remote possibility of going to sleep. Far from settling down, the energy coursing through my body had increased as the night went on, moving rhythmically up and down from head to toe. There was no doubt in my mind that it was orgone energy or whatever the hell name anyone wished to give it. It was like nothing I had ever felt before and I knew that I had tapped into the strongest force in the world. I sat by my window on the river, watching the debris float by. I thought about life and people and kids and sex and my ex-wife and psychoanalysis and how in the name of God human beings had gotten themselves into the shape they were in and finally, about five-thirty in the morning, I fell asleep.

FOUR

Twenty-four years prior to my departure from Dr. Baker's office that Tuesday, Wilhelm Reich had sat in his rented quarters in Oslo, Norway, and thought about coming to New York. He had been driven from his beloved Freud and from Vienna by a campaign of vilification spread by certain of his fellow analysts who had insinuated that he was a sex fiend. He had gone to Germany and worked there for a while but the rumors had started again: He was a communist or a fascist or a pervert, or all three. He had gone to Norway and continued his work but then World War II was about to explode. He decided to come to New York and he lived and worked in a house in Queens for a year but it began to close in on him so he bought a piece of land in Maine with room to breathe and an old building on it and he continued his practice and his experiments and his training of a handful of young psychiatrists to work in what he now called the science of orgonomy. (One of the young psychiatrists was Elsworth Baker.) He came to believe that orgone energy did not merely exist in the body but that it was all around us in the atmosphere and could be easily seen. He found that materials like wood or insulating wool tend to store up the energy, whereas it passes through metal. He thought the energy might prove to have natural healing powers if he could accumulate enough of it in a confined area, so he built a simple structure the size of a phone booth, made of alternate layers of metal and Celotex. This accumulator attracted the trapped orgone energy and a person could sit in it and feel a pleasant tingling sensation and possibly derive some health-giving benefits from nature's own energy. The accumulator was never an important part of Reich's work but his enemies called it his orgone box and said that people would sit in it and masturbate. They laughed at it and lied about it and used it to discredit him. They implied that Reich thought he had some kind of a magic box that would replace psychotherapy and you didn't even have to plug it into the wall.

When Reich worked with his patients they would usually take their clothes off so that he could observe their breathing and the tightness of their muscles. His enemies spread rumors that he indulged in orgies. They called him a pervert and a quack and a lunatic. Why? Because he dealt with man's nature on its deepest level, which inevitably enrages the little character assassins of the world who always seem to be around great men. They are the same ones who hounded Jesus, and D. H. Lawrence and Lenny Bruce. Somebody got to someone in the U.S. Food and Drug Administration (F.D.A.) and falsely said that Reich claimed his accumulator was a cure for cancer. F.D.A. ran some inept tests on the accumulator, said that it was worthless and got an injunction to prevent Reich's shipping it across state lines to other orgonomists. An assistant of his went ahead and shipped one anyway and the government issued a warrant for Reich's arrest. Instead of hiring a top-notch lawyer and fighting on legal grounds, Reich naively believed that if he simply talked about the importance of his work, justice would prevail in the United States of America. He was sentenced to two years in the Federal penitentiary and it was ordered that all his accumulators and other equipment be destroyed and his books burned. In the summer of 1956, F.D.A. agents entered Reich's property in Maine and smashed his equipment. They collected his books there and at the publishers in New York and they were burned in the city incinerator. This was twenty years after the Nazi book-burning in Germany.

Following several futile appeals, Reich entered the Federal penitentiary, first at Danbury, Connecticut, and then at Lewisburg, Pennsylvania. He served not quite eight months of his sentence in increasingly ill health and died there on November 3, 1957. He was one of the greatest men in the history of the human race. Hundreds of years from now people will marvel at how the world treated him when he was alive. Most people ignored him (the scientific community, for instance). Of the rest, they either hated him and tried to hurt him or they worshiped him. I don't know which is worse. He had a very few friends who did neither and one of them was A. S. Neill of Summerhill, who loved Reich and understood him.

24

Today, fourteen years after his death, road-company Reichs are springing up like toadstools. Esalen, Encounter and all the other seeing-feeling-touching-experiencing groups are direct descendants of Reich, although they rarely give him credit. Perhaps it's just as well. A weekend at Esalen, bathing in the nude with thirty or forty people, being massaged and stroked, or screaming your lungs out at your wife probably feels great but has about as much lasting therapeutic effect as an evening at the Garden with Billy Graham. In fact, it probably does a person harm by getting his hopes up for freedom and then being unable to deliver. False hopes breed frustration and hatred. The handful of medical orgonomists carrying on Reich's work today know the patience required and the dangers inherent in the work. His achievements and even his way of thinking were bound to be misunderstood by the vast majority of people in the world, because he had developed a "functional" system of thought as opposed to the traditional "mechanical" systems. This enabled him (or forced him) to look at the whole instead of the parts. For centuries doctors have studied the human being by dissecting dead bodies. Reich studied living ones. He tried to find out what life had in common with all other life. Classical science can split atoms and rearrange chromosomes. It can even go so far as to create life in a test tube but it refuses to concern itself with the question of what life *is*. It relegates this to the spiritual.

Reich refused to be bound by the rules. He wouldn't accept the traditional split between body and soul, instinct and intellect, psyche and soma. He worked with

25

his patients and he experimented in his laboratory and the more he did so, the more he found that his "thin red line of logic" would carry him into overlapping areas of science . . . from the psychological to the physical and back again. Gradually, it dawned on him that the whole idea of there being a split in man's nature had come about as a result of armoring. Because we tighten our muscles against our internal energy streamings which run from head to toe in a pleasurable way and make us feel unified, not just within ourselves but with the whole pulsating universe, we feel cut off and shut out like strangers in our own world.

We perceive nature (God, the universal spirit) in a once-removed way, through the wrong end of a telescope, and the whole idea of universality becomes imbued with mysticism. It becomes "us against them": man against the elements and the natural order of things. To think of ourselves as part of the overall scheme makes us feel like an insignificant speck in the cosmos, because we have destroyed our capacity to derive pleasure from being part of the whole. If people are locked in a dark dungeon for years, their eyes will lose their ability to tolerate light and they will eventually learn to hate the sun. Because Reich tried to make us see the truth about ourselves, we couldn't stand to have him around. It's bad enough to live in the bleak, miserable way we do without having someone rub our noses in it, especially when he tells us what we have to do to change and it terrifies us. Reich grabbed hold of the truth by the tail and it pulled him along over the God-damnedest road anybody ever traveled. He was hounded every step of the way by what he called the "emotional plague," which consists of certain highly energetic individuals, filled with rage and frustration because of their armored pelvises, who have an irrational need to seek out and attack healthy, loving, industrious life. "Emotional plague" people can't simply ignore decent, productive people, they have to try to destroy them the way antimatter would destroy matter. The mere existence of a man like Reich posed a mortal threat to the "emotional plague." It tried to drive him crazy and if it didn't succeed it's a miracle. Finally, it killed him.

It will continue to try to twist and warp his ideas the way it has twisted the ideas of all great and loving men. His belief in the basic decency of genitality will probably eventually be perverted into the Wilhelm Reich Free Fuck Society when the pornographic plague crowd manages to filter out all feelings of responsibility and tenderness. The truth is like TNT. It should have "handle with care" and "proceed at own risk" stamped on it. However, there's nothing else worth going after so, since Reich had prepared a roadmap, I figured I'd take the trip.

FIVE

The Wednesday morning after my first visit to Baker I woke up, after about five hours sleep, feeling exhilarated. My coffee tasted better than it ever had and even the garbage floating down the East River seemed to me to have a lightness and symmetry to it. The feeling lasted for the rest of the day. It was a sense of well-being and at-peace-with-the-world-ness. My body felt light and little ripples of pleasure rolled up and down my arms, legs and torso. When I breathed, the sensation of movement continued down into the base of my torso and it felt good. I felt vaguely horny in a tender way and the thought of women in general filled me with love. I went to the theater that night and did a performance that pleased me. I felt very much in contact with the other actors on stage and I could project myself into the character with no difficulty. I told Maureen and Mia and the others about my experience. I don't know what they

28

thought but they could see I was on top of the world. After the show I went to Dick Edward's bar for a while and then home to my apartment.

I was starting to unwind. The pleasurable ripples were lessening and a sense of anxiety was starting to take over. Brownish marks that would be black and blue by the next day began to appear on my body where Baker had pinched and gouged at me. I sat by the window with a drink in my hand and looked at the river. The moon shone brightly and I made out a wooden box floating by that said Del Monte on it . . . Del Monte *what* I wondered? Pears, maybe.

I got into bed, realized that I was cold and reached down to the foot of the bed for the extra blanket. Then it occurred to me that I was cold with fear. I tried to examine my feelings as I had learned to do in psycho-analysis. It was a different kind of dread than I had ever experienced before. I thought of a marionette show I had seen as a kid with skeleton puppets who danced to the music of the *Danse macabre* and then began to fly apart, with legs and arms and head coming off and ribs and pelvis coming apart. I felt like I too was starting to come apart. The anxiety was terrific and I was aware that I was involuntarily tightening up on my muscles to hold myself together. The wonderful joyous liberated feeling was going away and in its place was a sense of holding on for dear life. My armoring, if that's what it was, seemed like an old friend now. People say, "I'd rather die in the electric chair than spend my life in prison," but prisoners never say that. A life in chains is better than no life at all, except in theory.

29

I realized it was going to take all the courage I could muster to de-armor myself. I knew I would fight Dr. Baker every step of the way but I also remembered how I had felt for that thirty-six hours or so after my first treatment and I wanted it more than anything else in the world. I got through the night and the rest of the week and once again picked my way through the dog shit of Carl Schurz Park and past the mayor's house and into Baker's building.

I smelled the ozone in the hall, let myself in and strained to hear if the girl was in there crying again. After a while the door to the bedroom opened and I looked up from my magazine quickly enough to see a pretty young woman with a pale face streak into the bathroom. Baker came right out and told me to go in, which I did. He told me to take my things off and lie down on the cot again. I stripped to my terrible jockey shorts and my black socks (like they wear in a dirty movie, I thought) and lay down on the bed.

"What kind of a week did you have?" asked Baker and I told him. I heard the girl flush the toilet and leave.

"Your reaction of clamping down after a period of pleasurable sensations was completely natural and to be expected," he said. "You won't always have those nice feelings but it's important to remember what they were like so you can work towards them again. It will help you tolerate the fear you'll feel as your armor breaks down." He then told me to relax and breathe as deeply and easily as I could. I did so and he watched me for a little while and then he said, "Like most people, you breathe in easily enough but you're not breathing out fully," and with that he once again placed the palm of one hand on my chest and pushed down on it with his

30

other hand. For a slender man he had the strength of King Kong. I listened intently for the sound of cracking ribs. I would take a deep breath and Baker would force it out of me, pushing down and holding it till I was making rasping noises like Barry Fitzgerald doing a death rattle. However, when he stopped his pushing I found that I was able to continue the more or less deep breathing and I could feel the impulse of the expansion and contraction of my chest continuing down toward my pelvis. It felt good. "Now," said Baker, "continue the breathing and start the bicycle kicking again." I began the rhythmic kicking, lying there on my back, drawing my legs up and smacking my calves down, one after another, on the bed. Baker continued to remind me to breathe as I kicked and gradually that pleasant tingling sense of moving energy reappeared inside me. I kicked and kicked and breathed and breathed. My lips began to feel full and tingly and sensuous and my fingers felt filled with energy as if I could point one of them, like a *Marvel Comics* super-hero, and a ray would shoot out of it. The session came to an end and once again I walked out of Baker's office on a cloud.

For several weeks on Tuesdays at two, I breathed and kicked. (I have since found out that my chest and breathing were being worked on first to mobilize energy in my body, which would help in the de-armoring process. Energy is built up with the intake of air.) Baker now had me pounding with my fists on the bed as I kicked. I would pound and kick and breathe and the rhythm would take me over and I would be transported.

Then, one Tuesday, a terrifying thing happened: I began

to feel paralyzed. I had been doing my breathing and kicking routine when I noticed that my face and lips felt funny and my fingers began to flex like they had a Charley horse in them. I felt an almost painful sensation like someone had plugged me into the wall and turned on the juice. Then I couldn't move my face or arms at all and Baker stopped everything and began rubbing my hands and gradually I returned to normal. "What the hell was that?" I asked.

"You built up more energy than you could tolerate at this point," he said, "so your body contracted against it."

"Maybe it was too much oxygen from all that breathing," I said.

"No," said Baker, "that's what classical medicine would say it was, but you'll see . . . later on in your therapy you'll be able to breathe as much as you like without contracting."

Tuesdays came and went and when Baker felt that I had built up enough energy in my chest he began work releasing the chronically tightened muscles which controlled my eyes. This is the first segment of armoring which has to be freed in all patients. There are seven segments in all: the ocular (it's all-important to free the eyes), the oral (mouth, chin, throat, etc.), the cervical (the deep muscles of the neck, which hold back crying), the thoracic (the chest, which contains the emotions of heartbreak, bitter sobbing, rage and longing), the diaphragmatic (murderous rage is held in the diaphragm), the abdominal and the pelvic (disturbances of the pelvis can result in erective impotence, premature ejaculation and constipation; the pelvis contains anxiety and rage). The segments are always worked on in this order.

32

To start freeing my eye armoring, Dr. Baker held a pencil in front of me and told me to keep looking at it. He then moved it around quickly in random patterns which forced me to look about spontaneously. This would be kept up for what seemed like fifteen or twenty minutes and the results were amazing to me. My eyes felt free in my head and I could sense a direct connection between them and my brain. Then, he would have me roll my eyes about without moving my head, forcing them to focus on each wall in the room as their glance lit upon it. All the time I was doing this I would have to keep breathing deeply and rhythmically.

He would tell me to grimace and make faces (I felt like a fool). He would have me try to make my eyes look suspicious or attempt to get them to express longing. All of these things gradually made my eyes feel like they were being used again for the first time in many many years and it felt wonderful.

One day, in the midst of expressing longing, I suddenly thought about an old dog of mine. His name was Homer and I had gotten him when I was nine or ten from the Animal Rescue League in Boston. I had taken him home on the subway and we had fallen in love. He was a large, ungainly half-grown shepherd. I had rescued him from a cage and from death and he seemed to know it and no two creatures on earth had ever felt so close. We were together constantly and I always felt deliriously happy when I found him waiting for me after school. I would tie a rope around his neck and take him for long walks and then we would come home and spend what seemed like hours staring into each other's eyes. But Homer was a nervous dog and my parents were constantly afraid he would bite one of the neighborhood children. One day he nipped at my mother and my father called the Animal Rescue League and they sent a truck and took him away. I ran to my room and threw myself on my bed and sobbed for an hour. Then, I made a vow that no one would ever make me cry again, and I never did cry, not even when my mother died when I was in high school, until that day in Dr. Baker's office. Tears began to roll down my cheeks for the first time in twenty-five years. I lay on the bed there crying and then the hour was over and I walked through Carl Schurz Park and thought about Homer and I cried some more.

On the following Tuesday, instead of a pencil, Dr. Baker pulled out a fountainpen flashlight. He turned out the lights and shone it in my eyes and moved it around. It was a psychedelic effect. I followed it with my eyes as it made patterns in the dark and the effect was startling. I could actually feel the unlikely sensation of my brains moving in my head. Baker waved the flashlight around in front of me for about fifteen minutes and then he turned on the lights and looked deep into my eyes and said, "They're coming along nicely." Everything about the way he worked with me and the way he passed judgment on how I was responding was not mechanical but was the result of one human being's ability to put himself in touch with the feelings and energy charges of another.

"Make a face at me," said Baker and I turned on him with a stupid leer. "Now, accentuate it," he said. I twisted my face into a hideous gargoyle's expression. "What does it make you feel?" he asked.

"I dunno," I lied.

34

"It must make you feel something."

"Well, I guess . . . contemptuous."

"You guess?"

"Yes."

"You don't know?"

"All right, contemptuous."

"You feel contemptuous of me?"

"Well, I must, I suppose."

"You suppose?"

"All right, Goddamnit! I *do!*"

"Feel what?"

"Contemptuous! Jesus!"

"What's the matter?"

"I *told* you what I felt."

"But I didn't feel it from you."

"All right, dammit, it's a lot of crap . . . lying here rolling my eyes around."

"Stick your finger down your throat," said Baker.

"What?" I said.

"Gag yourself."

"But I'll throw up all over your bed."

"If you want to you can," he said. "Just keep breathing while you do it."

I lay there breathing deeply and stuck my finger down my throat and gagged. Then I did it again.

"Keep breathing," said Baker. My lower lip began to tremble like a little kid's, tears began to run down my face and I began to bawl. I sobbed for five minutes as if my heart would break. Finally, the crying subsided.

"Did anything occur to you?" asked Baker.

"I thought about my mother and how much I loved her

and how I felt like I could never reach her and I just felt hopeless and heartbroken," I said. "I felt like I was able to feel these things deeply for the first time since I was little, and it's such a relief to be able to cry and it isn't a lot of crap, I was just scared."

"Yes," he said. "It is frightening. You have a lot of anger to get out, a lot of hate and rage and then a lot of longing and a lot of love. Okay," he said, "I'll see you next time."

And I got up and got dressed and left.

SIX

"If the whole world is armored (including me)," I thought, "and basically incapable of sexual satisfaction, that's why everybody is always horny. But if it's true, how the hell did we all get that way?"

I found out what Reich thought about it one day, reading one of his books. It's only conjecture, but Reich figured that thousands of years ago in the caves, as early man began to perceive that he could perceive, he saw that nature was terrifying. He felt alone and helpless in the face of wind and storm and eruptions and predators. He also became aware of nature within himself in the form of gentle, pleasant, rhythmic stirrings. These were his orgonotic energy streamings. They were pleasurable and they made him feel at one with nature, but nature, when he thought about it (because he could), was a horrifying thing. So, he fought nature on the outside (to this day he tries to subjugate it to his will) and he rejected it on the inside, tightening his muscles against its gentle streamings the way a frightened man tenses up by holding his breath, and before long, the condition became habitual. In this way, the first man to armor himself may have done so and by doing so, he shut himself off forever from nature. The healthy, unarmored person, aware of the rhythmic, pleasurable pulsations within himself, feels a oneness with the farthest star and the nearest katydid because both he and they beat to the same rhythm. The armored person, having lost the ability to perceive his streamings, can only hypothesize intellectually about the unity of nature and his connection with it.

Armored man paid, of course, a terrible price for his armor. His natural, gentle softness changed into a hardness. Feeling out of touch with nature, he detested and feared it all the more. Having lost the ability to sexually self-regulate himself the way elephants and giraffes and mice do, he acquired secondary sexual characteristics. Where once he had taken his mate softly, tenderly, driven by a deep, primal urge to feel united with her, now the frustration caused by his inability to surrender and unite caused rage, a hammering at the door instead of a gentle slipping through it. The sexual drive began to seem to him like a cul-de-sac, a frustrating compulsion somehow still so terribly important to him, yet finally so unfulfilling, disappointing and disgusting. His sexual nature became cruel and perverse. This sickened him, in his better moments, so he covered his secondary layer of harsh, unnatural sexuality with a top layer of false "goodness" or "social decency." (It is this top layer that is being

38

stripped away today. The secondary layer can't be gotten rid of so easily.)

Time went by. Man continued his efforts to control and subjugate nature both without and within and he drove it farther and farther from himself. His armor came to mean security to him and he learned to love it, the way a prisoner loves his chains. His outer layer of "morality" would, in moments of drunkenness or lust, fade away to reveal the secondary layer of harsh hatefulness and he would rape and murder. This is the layer that Freud discovered and called the unconscious.

As man became more and more "civilized," erecting armored buildings and cities which further separated him from nature, he armored his children in his own image. He somehow sensed that an infant's fumbling attempts to reach its genitals had to do with the stirrings of nature within it and he forbade this. Cutting off the foreskin, as symbolically close as man could come to cutting out nature within himself, became a hallmark of "civilization" and the "uncircumcized dog" of an enemy was hated as unclean, inhuman and animal-like. Of course, he couldn't ever really drive nature out of himself but he could do his best to deny it. As man armored his child, it grew up frustrated, alternately submissive or rebellious, angry, fearful of its father but longing for his love, and slowly but surely there developed the great authoritarian-patriarchal tradition on which the western world is built. God, so close at hand to the unarmored person, so perceptible in the sweetness within one's own body and in the tender contact with the eyes and body of one's lover,

39

remained something unattainable, ever to be aspired to but never reached.

Back in the days when the Old Testament was being written, some poor, wretched, armored philosopher decided that man would have to die, would have to leave his body to find God. And really he was right. If we could just break out of the armor that has become part of us, surely God would be close at hand. So, the hope of someday shuffling off this mortal coil to get to God (oneness, unity, nature, contact, merger, union, love) became a way of tolerating an armored existence. And yet, somewhere deep down, man knew that he was one with God, that God was in him . . . so near and yet so far. The unattainable closeness became unbearable so he sent God away by mysticizing him. He built massive cathedrals, he organized crusades and wrested holy lands from infidels and excommunicated world populations; anything to blot out the fact that God was right inside him. And as the lovely tender natural sex drive atrophied in the body, the secondary drives took over. The desire to "break out" of the armor became a desire to thrust and pierce. Rape, or phantasies of rape, became a way of sexual life. Man linked sex with economics and power. He felt alone and miserable and afraid of God, whom he now perceived as an angry vengeful father (because when he was a small boy he had touched that forbidden little thing alone there in the dark and God, who knows all, must just be biding his time figuring out the right punishment). He tried to deny his animal mortality by establishing a family name and fortune that would live forever.

That meant grabbing more land than he needed (something a rhinoceros would never do), building himself an impregnable, cold, stone-towered place in which to live (something a bear would never do), sticking a chastity belt on his wife to insure that his seed would continue through his son, terrorizing the son to insure he'd "respect" his father and not slit his throat in the night, and finally, cementing the whole thing together with a powerful code of "morality" backed up by fear and force. Still, late at night, pacing the halls of his castle (or the dirt floor of his hovel) it all seemed meaningless and empty, even as it does today. He could build a castle or a cathedral and he could study the philosophers who tried to make life more bearable by intellectualizing a reason for existence but it's hopeless and late at night he knew it. The feeling of hopelessness stems from the frustration of the deep cosmic yearning for merger, union and oneness which can only be obtained through the unarmored, healthy capacity to melt into a loved one in full orgasm, lost forever to armored man.

Reich was once asked the age-old question, "What is truth?" and he answered, "To find your way to the thing you feel when you love dearly, or when you create, or when you give birth to your children, or when you build your home or when you look up at the stars at night." These are the things that we feel in common with every other human who is capable of feeling. They are the deepest, tenderest, most profound and exhilarating of feelings and the capacity to feel them is the capacity to be free.

41

But man, having fashioned himself a jail-like body, has imprisoned himself in jail-like cities and jail-like civilizations. Prisoners dream of freedom. They scheme about it and plan for it and once in a great, great while somebody actually escapes. But for most of the prisoners, escape is only a dream. In order to survive in jail, the prisoner needs his dream but he dare not dwell on it too much or life in jail becomes intolerable. Emotional survival in prison requires a careful balance between hope and resignation. Once in a while, a few sick and evil prisoners will start stirring up the others about how bad conditions are in jail. They will start preaching rebellion and revenge against the establishment (the guards and the warden). The older and wiser cons, knowing what will happen, try to discourage this idea of rebellion but the freedom spark, having been stirred up, is hard to extinguish. Hasty, meaningless plans are formulated, a guard is ambushed, keys are stolen, the warden's office is seized, rioting breaks out, guards are held hostage, mattresses are ripped up and burned, equipment is destroyed, a list of nonnegotiable demands is presented to the warden, a few people are killed, the riot runs its course and eventually things settle down. The prisoners return to their cells, the suspected ringleaders are put in solitary confinement and library and TV privileges are suspended. On the outside, outraged liberals debate penal reform and on the inside, life proceeds pretty much as it was, except for the lost privileges. Some of the cons feel more bitter than ever, most are indifferent, and a certain few sit on their bunks in the dark, remembering the revolt and grinning to themselves. And maybe the saddest thing

42

of all is that somewhere in the penitentiary, a prisoner who had carefully planned a well thought-out escape, who had manufactured a key or had had a gun smuggled in or arranged through a friend for a getaway car to be waiting by the west wall, or bribed a guard or dug a tunnel two-thirds of the way under the wall, is found out and thwarted because of the meaningless revolt of the hopeless band of rabble who never had a chance but were stirred up by the evil cons now sitting in their cells and grinning.

The prison that man has created for himself is stronger than any put up by governments. It's the prison of his own character structure and he recreates it in each of his children. There isn't going to be any mass-escape from it through political or social means. On the contrary, attempted mass-escapes have always resulted in more misery for the prisoners. Decent people, like the old wise cons, spend their lives trying to make life in the prison more bearable for their fellow inmates by fighting for reform. The hopped-up phoney breakout artists in our jail-world constantly need to surround themselves with a whirlwind of pseudo-revolutionary activity just to feel alive. That's their only motivation — to pump a few shivers of feeling into their dead bones. Real revolution is possible only if it begins on the inside and works its way out. Reich was one of the few true revolutionaries who ever lived and I had decided to join the revolution.

SEVEN

"Yell," said Baker one day as I lay on his bed of pain in my terrible Fruit of the Looms.

"What do you mean?" I said.

"Just yell," he said and I let out a feeble croak and then giggled. "Is that the best you can do?" he asked.

"Awk!" I replied and laughed again. He grabbed hold of the back of my head with one hand pushed my chin down my throat with the other with all his might. I was sure I'd look like Andy Gump for life.

"Jesus," I said when he finally let go.

"Now, let me hear you yell," said Baker. A loud sound came out of me that I was sure someone else had made.

"Again," he said and once more the marvelous ventrilo worked and a big noise came out of me.

"Turn over," he said and I flopped over and he began prodding at my back, around my shoulder blades. He found a spot he liked and began to press it. He pressed it

44

hard and I let out a howl. He squeezed and he pinched at it and I lay there and screamed. It occurred to me that I had never really screamed before, except maybe when I was a baby and I'm not even sure that New England babies scream. Screaming was something that actresses do in the movies. But the muscle that Baker had found did the trick. It wasn't that it hurt so much, although it did—it was that he had found the "on" button and I had no choice. At least, it seemed that way. The muscles he was loosening were the very ones which I had tightened up on so many years before when it had suited my purpose never to scream again. I had kept them tight for so long that the condition had become chronic and now Baker was unlocking them and all the leftover screams were pouring out. Finally, the governor sent a reprieve and Baker stopped gouging.

"Now," he said, "make a fist and hit the bed." I scrunched my hands together and pounded feebly at the sheet.

"Harder," said Baker. I felt like a simp. Suddenly he began gouging at that sore, knotted muscle again and he didn't stop, and then I really hit the bed. I began pounding hard with both fists, lying there on my stomach, yelling and screaming and biting and having a tantrum. I tried to beat my way through the bed to get away from his hands. I sobbed uncontrollably. I cried harder than I ever had before. Then Baker let me alone and I just lay there, sobbing deeply. Every time I took a breath, it felt like it went right down to the base of my spine and then I'd cry again—wracking, convulsive sobs. I cried for about five minutes and then I lay there with my face buried in the sheet for another five, involuntarily breathing those deep,

deep breaths. Finally, I recovered and turned over on my back.

"How do you feel?" asked Baker.

"I feel fantastic relief," I answered. "It's just great to be able to cry again after all these years, but there seems to be something missing. The feeling is incomplete. I also notice that there are very few tears when I cry."

"The hard emotions have to come out first," said Baker, "the rage and the fury and the hate. Only when they're released can you get through to the tender feelings—the love and longing and sadness. Your crying is angry crying right now."

On Tuesday after Tuesday Baker jabbed at me. He found muscles where I didn't know they existed and they were all tight, tense and knotted. He knew just which ones to look for and what they were holding in and what to do to make them let go. It hurt like hell and it became a way of life with me to be absolutely covered with black and blue marks. I'm sure that the people at the theater, when they saw me change in the dressing room, thought I had fallen into the clutches of a sadomasochistic weirdo. As Baker jabbed and pinched and dug, I howled. I screamed and ranted and shrieked and clawed at the bed. I sobbed and pounded and beat. I rolled my eyes and shook my head and carried on like a lunatic. And every time, the sessions would end with my breathing impulses going deeper and deeper down my body until I could feel them in my feet.

I would leave his office with the energy coursing around in me like the lights on a pinball machine. The bald guy with the *Life* magazine would look up and say hello now and I would go out through the lobby of the building past the man at the reception desk who looked at me strangely and out into the air. Baker's building was smack down on the river and if you had to be in New York it was as nice a place as you could find. That's why old man Gracie built his mansion there in 1799 and that's why the mayor lives in it now. When I came out of the office, I would always look up at the sky to see if I could spot the tiny dancing points of light which Reich had said were vesicles of orgone energy. The way they moved in and out and around each other seemed almost playful to me and it always made me smile when I saw them. On Tuesday nights I could always count on staying up till close to dawn because the energy in me was like a hundred cups of coffee.

I'd wake up in the morning and gag myself in the bathroom, running the water and flushing the toilet to cover the noise so sweet Bridie wouldn't think the master was heaving his guts out in the sink. Baker had told me that "eliciting the gag reflex" (sticking your finger down your throat) relieved anxiety and was something I could do with beneficial results every A.M. for the rest of my life. It does work, strange as it sounds (as long as you keep breathing), and you never throw up but you always feel foolish if anyone's around. He also told me to look directly into my eyes in the mirror while shaving each morning and try to see what the expression in them was. It's amazing how nervous this makes you feel but if you can stand to look at yourself for a while for some reason it does reduce anxiety. My life settled into a routine: *Never Too Late*, Dr. Baker and Dick Edward's bar.

Then I found Carolyn. I had been looking for her for some time then, never knowing who she might be and

47

taking out girl after girl who wandered unknowingly into Edward's. None of them, of course, was Carolyn, although I had no way of knowing that at the time and did what I had to. Bridie was very understanding of the procession of wood nymphs who passed in and out of my life and apartment. One night Michael McCourt, my friend and bartender from Dick Edward's, allowed as how the next night, Friday, was his night off and proposed that he introduce me to the joys of an uptown establishment named Spark's Pub. The ensuing eve, Good Friday, he picked me up at the theater and we cabbed up to Eightieth Street and York and entered a dark crypt with I.R.A. posters on the walls and a jet-black men's room. When my eyes became accustomed to the gloom I saw the most breathtaking girl in the western world sitting at a table with another cute girl and a fellow. I slugged down two or three beakers of Spark's bar scotch and moved over to play the jukebox, which was next to their table. She had on a fuzzy yellow sweater and she was possessed of an almost patrician beauty which made you want to take her home, rip off her clothes and ravish her.

"How do you do?" I said and my eyes turned glassy so I couldn't see if she smiled or sneered. Having deposited my quarter in the jukebox, I moved back to the bar. Michael McCourt knew Don Spark, the genial boniface of the crypt who, it turned out, knew Carolyn. He took me over to her table and introduced us. My orgone energy raced around like a dozen Bakers were pounding on me and before the evening was over, my fate was sealed.

I don't know whether it was falling in love with Carolyn or the fact that Dr. Baker began working on my diaphragm

48

muscles, but I suddenly started to get those insanely delirious streaming sensations again. They were like a soft spring breeze blowing through me and they made me feel an awareness of my body in 3-D. They seemed to be restricted mostly to the upper part of me but they felt wonderful and I was grateful for them. Dr. Baker kept on trying out different methods of having me get rage out. One day he handed me a sheet folded and rolled up like a baseball bat and asked me if I would like to hit the bed with it. I sat back on my heels and used the rolled-up sheet like a carpet beater, smacking the be-Jesus out of the bed. It felt great. He told me to make different sounds as I hit, so I did. I growled ferociously or made sadistic grunts or various noises that sounded vaguely sexual to me. I would smash and smack at the bed until I felt completely exhausted and just couldn't go on anymore. Then he would have me do the old bicycle kick and the arm pounding, lying on my back and flailing about like an infant having a tantrum in its crib. The breathing and the rhythmic pounding would transport me and I would become an infant again and get the old tantrums out of my system. As the freeing of my armor proceeded systematically down towards my pelvis, I began having deeply meaningful dreams at night which I would describe to Dr. Baker but which I found I was very often able to spontaneously analyze myself. I no longer worried about getting paralyzed, since my system could now tolerate its increased energy level with no difficulty.

Deep feelings of heartbreak and longing started to pour out of me which I had never been able to get anywhere near in my ten years of psychoanalysis. Baker would tell me to reach out my arms longingly and just the act of doing so could bring back a flood of deeply tender memories of my mother and of the frustrations I had felt as a child.

My crying now began to change in quality. Having worked through my stored-up rage, fury and hatred to the point where I could express them fully and get them out of my system, the deeper layer of soft feelings emerged. My anger at the childhood affronts (real or otherwise) which I felt I had suffered at the hands of my parents went away. My feelings of hatred for my mother for the rejection I had felt by her faded and what I now felt was tender, longing love. But since she was no longer here and because I'm not a kid anymore anyway, the love turned to heartbreak. One day, lying on Baker's bed, I thought about my mother's dying and I sobbed and sobbed. I felt for his hand and he let me hold it and he stroked my arm and comforted me. When I had finished crying, I got dressed and walked out of the building and crossed over to the river and stood for a long time looking down at it and realized that I had finally, twenty years after my mother's death, bid her good-bye.

EIGHT

"God," I thought to myself one day, "are there any people on earth who aren't armored?" and it occurred to me that here and there, for no apparent reason, there are people who, in spite of the usual rotten upbringing that most of us are subjected to, emerge relatively unscathed and quite naturally healthy. Culturally, nearly all civilizations force their children to armor. One of the few exceptions seems to be the Trobriand Islands in the South Pacific. In 1929 Wilhelm Reich's friend Bronislaw Malinowski, the famous anthropologist, published his classic book, *The Sexual Life of Savages,* which was about the two years he had spent in those islands. No one knows for sure what the human race would be like if it were as true to its nature as, say, tigers and elephants and cockroaches are to theirs, or what kinds of civilizations it would have developed. But the Trobriand Islanders apparently come as close to being natural as any people on earth.

51

There are two things that seems to be the basic needs of all humans: work and love. "Natural" people, in touch with their instinctual needs, would build a civilization which would facilitate the gratification of those needs. The Trobriand Islanders seem to have done just that. There is full sexual freedom for people of all ages from infancy on up. Children engage unashamedly in happy, healthy, normal sex play of the kind suitable to their age. This sex play is not merely tolerated by the community but is affirmed as completely normal behavior.

As in our culture, there is a goodly amount of self-segregation between the sexes. Bands of boys, aged eight or nine, will wander off on expeditions into the woods in pursuit of rough-and-tumble boys' activities. They'll go camping or swimming or rock collecting, sometimes staying away for days. Nobody worries about them; they don't go until they feel ready to do so and when that happens, it means they *are* ready. Meanwhile, the girls are in their own groups, engaged in girls' play. Suddenly, the boys swoop down on the girls. To attack them? No. They have collected wildflowers and pretty shells and stones and they have come to give them to the girls. The sex play is not harsh or strident. There is no need to play doctor or to use any other excuse for intimate contact; it comes completely naturally. The boys and girls pair off and lie in the grass or on the beach, softly caressing each other and overflowing with love. When it is time, the love play is over and the boys are off on another exclusively male adventure, leaving the girls to themselves.

When they reach their teens, love becomes practically

52

their whole concern. Couples form and separate and come together again as they go about the business of searching for partners. The tribe provides a "longhouse" where the teen-agers can go and live. Even though the house is only one large room, fifteen or twenty couples may be making love in it, on a given evening, with complete privacy. This is hard for us, with our sex-starved natures, to comprehend but to a Trobriand teen-ager it would be an unthinkable breach of etiquette to intrude on another couple's privacy by looking at or listening to them. Moreover, he isn't interested. From infancy, the Trobriand teen-ager has observed human sexual behavior in all of its natural forms. It has been part of his life-experience and his education, so it holds no unhealthy fascination for him.

To imagine how strange our attitude toward sex would seem to a Trobriand Islander, picture a mythical society where eating is taboo. In such a society, everyone would, of course, eat, but they would do so secretly. Deprived of the chance to observe people eating in a relaxed and normal fashion, a child who grew up in such a society would have terribly mixed feelings about his need for sustenance. He would seize a piece of food and run to a hiding place to wolf it down, fantasizing that someone was eating with him. He would be racked with guilt about his fantasies and this would keep him from really enjoying the food. He would have trouble with his digestion. Late at night, when he was supposed to be asleep there would be a light on in the dining room (what a disgusting phrase) and his mommy and daddy would be in there alone . . . eating. The little boy would strain his ears to hear

53

what he could and then fall asleep fitfully. From other children, perhaps slightly older, he would hear tales of five-course dinners attended by several couples! He would listen to descriptions of rare and exotic foods and of the kinds of people who like to eat them. There would be whispered stories and jokes about food and eating and when they got angry, people would insult each other by saying things like "Go chew a steak!" and "You eat soup in public!" A young boy growing up in such a society would perhaps hear tales of countries like America, where there was "freedom to eat" and an unashamed attitude toward the appetite. But he would no more be able to imagine an American's nonchalance at dining in a restaurant than we could properly picture the atmosphere in the teen-agers' longhouse in the Trobriand Islands.

On moonlit nights in the islands, groups of young couples leave the longhouse. Older married people smile as they watch them stroll past, heading for a nearby beach. They build a fire and cook their dinner. They swim and dance and laugh and pick flowers and tell stories and then, couple by couple, they pair off and retire to make love under the moon. There are no fantasies or anxieties or guilts but only softness and tenderness and sensuality. Time goes by and a couple finds that they enjoy being together more than they enjoy being with anyone else. They are starting to be of an age where to be married carries with it status and the approval of the tribe. They announce their intentions. There is joy in the community and preparations are made for the wedding celebration. There will be feasting and dancing and a site will be chosen where the whole village will help with the construction of a house for the happy couple. Such meaningful work is welcomed by the people. When the ceremony takes place there are no vows of eternal fidelity, for as the young man and woman gaze deep into each other's eyes they know with every fibre of their bodies that they have no desire to touch or even look lustfully at anyone else. There is no word for promiscuity in the Trobriand language; the concept does not exist. The couple marries and enters into the adult life of the community. They have a baby. It would be shameful not to. It would be equally shameful for a girl to have a baby without being married. These tribal taboos, if you can imagine it, have nothing to do with attitudes toward sex because the Trobrianders don't believe that sex has anything to do with babies. They believe that sex is the gods' gift to men and women for their pleasure and happiness. They believe quite separately, that the gods send babies to a woman, once she is married, so that the tribe can grow and prosper and flourish. The baby arrives on a large leaf carried in on the tide on moonlit nights and enters the woman's body through a tiny hole on the top of her head. Once inside, the baby grows and nine months later emerges as a source of joy to one and all. The husband has nothing to do with it. When Malinowski tried to point out the connection between sexual intercourse and babies to the islanders, they roared with laughter. To show the absurdity of his claim, they cited the example of a village chieftain who had been away on a long trip to another island for almost two years. Upon his return home, he was delighted to have his wife present him with a six-month-old son. Since it was obvious that the man could not have had relations with his wife while he was away, this proved that there could be no connection between sex and babies. Unable to refute such logic, Malinowski could merely sit wondering to himself about the obvious question: If the islanders don't believe in the relationship between sexual intercourse and birth, they obviously feel no need to take precautions and yet pregnancies outside of wedlock were virtually unheard of. One old man thought he remembered a case years back, of an unmarried girl who had given birth. It had been generally assumed that the gods were furious with her for some reason and she and her child had been driven in disgrace from the town. Malinowski realized that either something magical was happening or the islanders were lying and had some extraordinary and practically foolproof method of birth control. In the two years he spent with them, he became convinced that the Trobrianders were not lying and that somehow their young women, in touch with their feelings and bodies and emotions, simply didn't become pregnant when it wasn't socially acceptable to do so, and did when it was. Is this really so hard to believe? Nowadays, we know more and more about the relationship between psyche and soma and about unconscious emotional control over bodily functions. Everyone has heard stories about the married couple who try for years and years to have a child, finally give up and adopt a baby, whereupon the wife immediately conceives. Conceivably the young woman on the Trobriand Islands, not having messed up the delicate balance in their systems as we have, are so in touch with themselves that their state of arousal is affected by their state of fertility. Maybe there's some other reason.

One of the things that breeds promiscuity, wife-swapping and extramarital cheating in our civilization is the concept of lifelong compulsive monogamy. The Trobrianders, not having armored themselves in the first place, have never lost touch with their original sweet true sexuality. Since they have not denied this primary layer of sexual behavior, it has not turned into the hard, cruel, secondary layer and, in turn, they don't need the third, cover-up layer of "Thou Shalt Not" to keep themselves in tow. They don't need and they don't have lifelong compulsive monogamy. Neither do they have marital cheating, which is a by-product of compulsive monogamy. Love affairs and marriages last as long as love lasts and that may be for many, many years. But the point is that while they do last, they are sources of happiness. They never degenerate into compulsive, hate-filled "duty." A bitter, loveless marriage in which a person's life wastes away never continues "for the sake of the children." What does happen to the children when a marriage breaks up? The Trobriand Island society is a matriarchy as opposed to our western culture, which is a patriarchy. This means that family wealth (land, etc.) passes down through the mother as opposed to the father. This does away with economic inheritance as a need for a marriage to remain insoluble. No matter how many husbands a woman has had, her children's inheritance, whatever it may be, comes to them upon the death of their mother.

Regarding the emotional problems that a child has when his parents' marriage breaks up, these are vastly

57

diminished in the Trobriand Islands. First of all, the whole tribe (his mother's) is his family. From birth, the "fatherly" duties of guidance (moral, financial, educational, providing a model to imitate, etc.) are assumed by the maternal uncle. He, of course, remains constant no matter how many husbands the mother may have in the course of her lifetime. Before you start feeling sorry for the husband, thinking that he is left out of things, remember that he too is an uncle, obliged to love and instruct his sisters' children. Also remember that the Trobrianders don't believe that sexual intercourse, hence men, have anything to do with procreation. A husband may, and probably will, adore his wife's baby. He may play with it, hold it, sing to it, stroke it and as it grows up become great friends with it. But its maternal uncle is the "father-figure" in its life and that uncle has nothing to do with the romantic involvements of its mother. The husband is a loving friend and even after the break-up of a marriage, the friendship of a child and its unknowing father may continue quite unaffected by the end of the marital arrangement.

Don't get the idea from all this that Trobrianders take marriage lightly. Relationships formed are deep and lasting and not given up easily but one's first duty is to one's own life and the Trobriand society, having been set up by people who realize this, facilitates the pursuit of love, happiness and freedom, rather than restricting it. One last word about the Trobriand set-up. When a girl has a baby, her desire to love and laugh and sing in the moonlight doesn't pack up and go away. This is where the old people of the tribe come in. What more natural function for them than that of baby-sitter? How loved and appreciated they are for being there to watch the children when the young parents are off having fun. How needed they are and how needed they feel. They sit together, of an evening, the grandparents, and smile as they watch the younger people of all ages go past. A young couple may stop and talk with them for a moment and admire the baby they're minding and then bid them good night and go off about their business of seeking out happiness. The old folks sit in front of their huts content in the twilight of their full, rich lives, looking at the young people so much like they once were.

The relaxed and lovely naturalness of the Trobrianders is something we can only look at with wonder. We can never be like them and if we try to be, we'll only manage to make ourselves into grotesque imitations of them, like loonies at Bedlam mimicking the outsiders. What we can aspire to is to be the best of our kind of people. To do that we've got to know exactly what we are and that's what I was in the process of finding out on Tuesdays with Baker.

NINE

Dr. Baker and I were working our way down the segments of my armoring. One day he said to me, "Turn over and hit the bed with your pelvis."

"What do you mean?" I said.

"Just do it," said Baker, and I rolled onto my stomach and began arching my back and banging my groin down onto the bed. My whole pelvic area felt stiff and inflexible.

"Try to move your pelvis separately from the rest of you," said Dr. Baker. He pushed his hand down hard in the small of my back and held my spine immobile.

"Now hit with your pelvis," he said. I tried again and although it was an effort my pelvis moved more by itself now. As I waggled it up and down I could feel an anger overtaking me. I didn't know what I was mad about but I knew I was starting to feel furious. Then I really got pissed off. Baker found a spot on my ass (gluteus maximus) about two inches to the right of my spine and he pressed

60

it and I hit the roof. I began pounding and kicking and hitting and screaming and carrying on like a trapped scorpion. He wouldn't quit pressing on it and his thumb felt like a hot poker. I squawked and cursed and bawled and wondered how I'd have any voice left to go on at the theater that night. Finally he let up and I lay there with my face pressed into the sheet and cried. When I got up and got dressed to go home, my whole lower back felt like it had had steel wool sewn into it. The muscles ached and hurt and I felt frightened.

"I feel scared as hell," I said as I buttoned up my shirt and tied my tie.

"Yes, you will," he answered. "The pelvis, when it's armored, holds in the deepest rage and fears. Your anxiety is a good sign, though. Anxiety means movement and movement means life. Just stick it out."

I called up Carolyn and went over to her apartment. She and her roommate, Sheila, the cute girl she had been with that night in Spark's Pub, lived in a fancy building on Park Avenue and Eighty-sixth Street. Whoever had designed the building had wound up with an absurd little space on each floor between the two service elevators. The building was a co-op but of course no one wanted to buy accomodations with a living room 15 by 9, a bedroom so narrow you practically had to sleep standing up and a double exposure, each looking onto a separate air shaft. These quarters were euphemistically called an apartment and offered for rent . . . cheap. Carolyn and Sheila, poor as churchmice, had heard about the place, signed a lease, moved in and become the building's mascots. The rest of the place was populated by rich ladies with blue hair and

61

when these two bubbly young girls would bounce through the lobby and head back toward the service elevator the faces of the doormen would always break into smiles.

Thursday in New York is bulk pick-up day. Large items like no-longer-loved armchairs are left out on the sidewalk to be removed by the sanitation department. Members of that organization are not adverse to turning a fast buck by selling choice bits of reclaimable refuse to rent-poor secretaries and the like and Carolyn and Sheila had so furnished their tiny nest.

I took the service elevator up to the eleventh floor and rapped on Carolyn's door. When she opened it, I flopped into her Bulk Pick-Up Armchair. Carolyn was a dressmaker. She had her own sparse clientele and she worked out of the apartment. She stood there at the ironing board wearing blue jeans and a shirt and looking beautiful. I had tried to explain to her about Reich and Baker and why I was always covered with black and blue marks and why I made strange noises in the bathroom and why I couldn't sleep on Tuesdays. She was sweet and understanding but I knew she secretly wondered if I weren't sneaking over to Staten Island every Tuesday for a black mass or something.

One time I talked her into going to Dr. Baker. He spent a few sessions with her and said, "There's not much I can do for you. You're healthy." She's one of those rare people who emerge, for some reason, relatively unscathed. Maybe health was in her genes. She had always needed love and she told me once that at the age of fifteen she had remarked to her boyfriend that what they taught in church had to be wrong because she couldn't believe that God would be against pleasure.

Anyway, I looked at her with her glowing face and her beautiful body and her wonderful sense of ease and I knew I loved her deeply but I also felt this fear and rage pounding up out of my pelvis, out of my cock and balls and spine and entrails. Then, the anger turned to a stubbornness and I stood up and walked over to her at the ironing board and took her in my arms and held her tight and I felt her energy flow into my energy. My fear and anger drained away and I felt a stirring in my old stiff pelvis and it didn't feel so old and stiff anymore. It was a little more than two years now since I had first gone to see Dr. Baker and I felt profoundly changed. Not just more understanding but deeply different. I knew I was in the stretch now with my therapy. I knew it from the way I felt and I knew it because I knew Baker wouldn't have been working on my pelvis until all the other segments of armor had been freed. I felt capable of really loving, at least some, for the first time in my life. I realized that what passes for love in the overwhelming majority of cases is fear, anxiety or need for control. I felt connected with life, the earth and the universe in a quiet way that made me see a lot of things more clearly. And at that moment I felt horny. Luckily, Sheila worked days.

Week after week, Baker banged at my pelvis and I banged at the bed. He gouged at the muscles in my inner thighs (I hated this worse than anything in the therapy) and I kicked and I breathed. The deep breathing, which

63

lasted the duration of the treatment, was to build up the health-giving energy. It is this push-out of the energy, combined with the breaking down of the armor, which finally produces health. I now started to feel those wonderful pleasurable streamings again. Now they ran from head to toe and they made me feel grateful to be living. I also felt, sometimes, more frightened than I have ever felt in my life.

My pelvis began to feel alive and only as it did so was I able to see how dead it had felt before. As this last armored area started to be freed I became aware of what Reich meant by the unity of the body. When finally Baker had finished jabbing and gouging and pressing and watching and feeling and caring and my armor was broken down and gone, the battle still wasn't over. Now that I was theoretically capable of surrendering to the orgasm reflex, I felt little else but fear. Like a prisoner released after thirty years in the pen, I could only, pale faced, blink at the sun and, clutching my new suit to myself, move cautiously out into the world. Reich calls this "orgasm anxiety" and it's really at the seat of everyone's problems. The only cure for it is to learn to tolerate it and hope that it will diminish.

One day I ran frantically into Baker's office to tell him I could feel my heart pounding and moving around in my chest.

"Good," he said, "that's a sign of health. The heart pounding is anxiety, of course, but the fact that you are so in touch with your internal organs, that you feel them move, is healthy. I've had patients who could actually feel their brains moving."

64

My work on Tuesdays became just to breathe and take cognizance of my feelings and learn to tolerate the anxiety, and anxious as I was, I felt better than I ever had in my life.

Carolyn and I would go for long walks in the park on weekends and look up into the sky to see the little units of orgone energy tumbling and popping around in the atmosphere. I had told her that if she relaxed her vision they'd be apparent to her and they had been so immediately. Every kid sees them but when he asks what they are he is told that there is nothing there—it's only in his eyes.

I seemed to have inexhaustible energy and boundless optimism. I knew I was on the road to health and, late at night, in the furthest reaches of my megalomaniacal mind, I dreamed of taking the rest of the world with me. Having learned what I had learned I felt the pressing need that a religious convert or a reformed alcoholic feels to spread the faith. It seemed to me, as it once had to Wilhelm Reich, that the only hope for the human race lay in its children. The rest of us are too set in our ways and largely beyond salvation.

I began to look at children in the street with an odd light in my eyes. More than once I caught an alarmed mother watching me stare at her child in the street with messianic fervor . . . one more nutcake in the streets of New York. A wild idea began forming in the recesses of my mind and one day it bubbled to the surface.

TEN

It was a bright winter Sunday morning and Carolyn was in my apartment making brunch. I had been sitting holding a Bloody Mary and staring at a pamphlet which had been sent to me by Women's Strike for Peace. It was a beautifully put-together thing which said, in effect, that if we don't stop having wars we'll blow ourselves up.

"You've got to get to the kids," I mumbled.

"What?" yelled Carolyn out of the kitchen.

"If there's ever going to be a change in human nature so that we don't have wars, you've got to get to the kids," I said. "I think maybe I ought to start a school."

Carolyn walked out of the kitchen holding a panful of eggs.

"What do you know about running a school?" she asked.

"Nothing," I said. "But I can learn. Have you ever heard of the book *Summerhill?*"

"It's about that school in England, isn't it?"

66

"Yes," I said. "Well, a few years ago, somebody asked me to do a benefit. It was a girl named Margot Moser, who was in *My Fair Lady*. It was for something called the Summerhill Society to raise money to start a school or something. Anyway, I did the benefit and she gave me a copy of *Summerhill*. It's about this school in England where kids don't have to go to class or anything. I read the book and at first I disagreed with it wildly, but after a while it won me over. I joined the society, which had been set up by Harold Hart, the man who published the book. The society was supposed to start a school here like Neill's . . . that's the old guy who runs this school in England and wrote about it . . . A. S. Neill. But all we did in the society was meet and talk and I just realized the other day that they're never going to start a school. Maybe it's just as well. Do you know what the definition of a camel is?"

"No, what?" said Carolyn.

"A horse put together by a committee," I answered. She laughed. The sweet thing always laughs at my stuff.

"So I think I'll start one. I've got all this money I've saved from the run of the show and I could put a down payment on a building with it."

"O.K. If you want to," said Carolyn. I knew she wanted me to marry her and here she was agreeing that I should throw my money away on a hare-brained thing like a school if that was what I wanted.

"What's the Summerhill School about?" said Carolyn.

"Well," I said, "Neill is an old guy now, in his eighties. He started the school in 1927. It's a boarding school and he runs it on a principle he calls 'freedom without license.'

67

This means 'do your own thing but don't interfere with anyone else's.'"

"But doesn't that kind of permissive education just raise spoiled brats?" said Carolyn.

"It's not permissive," I said. "Look. In an authoritarian situation, bad behavior on the part of a kid is legislated out of existence . . . he's sent to the dean's office. In a permissive situation, the teacher or the parent pretends the bad behavior isn't annoying. Under 'freedom without license,' the kid has freedom but he's expected to behave responsibly. He has to earn his freedom by being able to handle it in a way that respects other people's rights."

"But isn't Summerhill a school for disturbed children?" asked Carolyn. She was putting the bacon and eggs on the table now. I walked over and sat down with her. It was Bridie's day off and Michele was out visiting her grandmother in Connecticut.

"Not really," I answered. "It just sort of became that because nobody wanted to send their kids to Neill's school except people who were desperate because their little darlings had been kicked out of three schools in a row. Also, Neill is a genius and a natural psychologist and he knows how to help kids. He studied with Reich, you know."

"No, I didn't know that," said Carolyn.

"Well, the American publisher of *Summerhill* cut Neill's references to Reich out of the book for some reason. Anyway, the kids who came to Neill came with a tremendous chip on their shoulders against school, teachers, parents and everybody else so Neill had to undo all that damage before he could begin to educate them positively. So, he had weekly meetings where kids and teachers could air their grievances and laws could be passed by majority vote." I was babbling on now, talking with my mouth full and Carolyn was beginning to catch my enthusiasm.

"Listen," I said, "he had kids who went for years without ever going to a class, but when they finally decided to go, they caught up with the other kids in less than a year. It's all a question of motivation. Make a kid sit at a desk all day and you're sowing the seeds of rebellion. Give him reasonable, rational choices and sooner or later a kid is going to elect to learn, probably sooner. Look at babies—they crawl when they could just sit there, they walk when they could keep on crawling, and they teach themselves to talk. Do you realize what an incredibly complex feat that is? Nobody teaches them, they teach themselves by observation. All of this tremendous energy is part of a child's built-in desire to learn and then society does everything it possibly can to stultify it. It makes a kid sit at a desk all day and raise his hand to go to the john and it tells a kid he can only be interested in certain things at certain times and that he *must* be interested in these things or he can't learn anything else." I was wolfing down the eggs. "God," I said, "I hated every waking moment of school from kindergarten on up. I spent my life trying to drive the teachers crazier than I felt they were trying to drive me. Any decent kid has to try to subvert such a system; it's the only way he can preserve his integrity. The kids who knuckle under become fags or milksops. I spent half of my childhood in the dean's office and I'm proud of it. Why the hell can't there be a school that lets a kid learn what the hell he wants when

69

he wants and at the same time teaches him that he has to respect other people's rights. The truth of the matter is that the reason so few people do respect other people's rights is that they never had their rights respected as a kid. Kids are the most brutalized minority in the world."

I was up and pacing wildly around the room now. "People lie to their kids a hundred times a day," I said, "and then they're amazed when the kids turn on them. If you tell a kid that Coke is bad for him and then he sees you drinking it, how the hell can you trust him alone in a bathroom with the iodine? You can't. So kids never do get trusted and they never learn to become trustworthy."

"So what are you going to do?" said Carolyn.

"Look," I said. "Everybody in the world can't go to Dr. Baker. I could and I really feel that I owe something for it. It's like if you find a well in the desert and you drink from it, you should put some water back in the primer bucket when you get through. As far as I can see, a school like Summerhill is preventive medicine and maybe if a kid went to one, he wouldn't need Baker when he grew up. I've got thirty-five grand saved. That's the amount the society was trying to raise to put a down payment on a building. I'll take it and buy one myself and I'll get the Summerhill Society's mailing list and send out a notice that I intend to start a school and we'll have a meeting of interested parties right here a week from Sunday." I hugged and kissed Carolyn in the excitement of it all and she laughed and we sat down and started looking through the real estate section of the *Times* for a suitable building.

The next day I called up the Summerhill Society and

they mailed me a list of the names and addresses of five hundred people in the New York area who had written to them expressing interest and we sent out a letter announcing a meeting. A friend of mine told me about a real estate lady, a dame by the name of Sugar Cane. I called her up and she said that, among the other buildings she knew of that were for sale, there was a fireproof union hall on Fifteenth Street. The asking price was $87,500, and she thought they would take thirty-five thousand down. Carolyn and I went with Sugar Cane to look at the building. It was perfect. The union was a little left-wing outfit called the Teachers' Union, no connection with the big one. It had served its purpose, having been very militant in its day and having forced the big AFL outfit, it felt, to take stronger positions. The three or four people who ran it now were old, gray-haired and tired of the struggle and the union was being disbanded. There were stacks of pamphlets everywhere, the curse of the left-wing, proclaiming solidarity of the workers and condemning the capitalist system. There were classrooms, where, no doubt, Karl Marx and John Dewey had been debated and a large assembly hall which would double as a gym for us. Carolyn and I looked through the building with Sugar Cane. It was incredibly dingy, with dark green paint throughout. The union seemed to have had an absolute mania for security and there were locks and keys everywhere and bars and iron gates and electric eyes. Carolyn and I looked at each other and nodded.

"I'll take it," I said to Sugar Cane.

"But don't you want to see some others?" she said.

"No," I said. "This will be fine."

71

My lawyer arranged a meeting, the papers were drawn up and signed and just like that, the building was ours.

About thirty people showed up at my house for the initial Sunday meeting. I had called Carolyn, and Bridie served coffee while Michele played with the two or three kids who had been brought along. I told the people of my intention to purchase the building, and of the several calls I had received from potential teachers. There seemed to be a feeling of genuine interest so we agreed to have a second and hopefully larger meeting in the auditorium of the new school building. Phone calls started to pour in during the days that followed. I met with teacher after teacher, all of whom were interested in working in a Summerhillian environment and willing to take short money in order to do so. I decided on a husband and wife team, a young couple named Rachel and Wilbur Rippy, and a young woman to run the nursery-kindergarten, named Renee Davis.

We had a big meeting a few weeks later in the auditorium of the new school building/old union hall. About a hundred people showed up. They poked their way through the dusty rooms of the four-story edifice and listened to the teachers and me talk about what kind of a school we planned to open. We told them that the school would be similar to Summerhill but that it would be a day school, open from 9 A.M. to 3 P.M. instead of a boarding school. We explained that attendance at class would be completely voluntary and that the children would have freedom to move about the building so long as they respected other people's rights and didn't race

72

up and down the stairs or otherwise endanger their health and safety.

At that point I really had grandiose ideas about saving the world by producing a crop of "super-babies" or "children of the future" who would lead the human race out of its destructive ways. I guess my wild-eyed enthusiasm was infectious because twenty sets of parents signed up their kids on the spot for the new school, which was to open in September of that year. I applied for and received a provisional charter from the New York State Board of Regents (three years later we were granted a permanent charter). The teachers ordered equipment; we swept and painted and knocked down walls. We named our enterprise The Fifteenth Street School, put up a sign, painted the front door bright yellow and settled in to wait for September.

ELEVEN

One night we lay in each other's arms and we found the courage not to fantasize or pretend, not to think of anyone or anything, not even to think "Here we are, it's us." We hadn't planned it; as a matter of fact, it was a night when we were rather tired and distracted and had thought of nothing except sleep. But suddenly our eyes met and something in us melted. We reached out to each other and touched and it was as if layers of us fell away. We moved closer and it was like two separate energy fields fusing into one. There was a wonder about it, a wonder about how we felt different to each other than we had before, physically different, an actual difference to the skin tone. And our eyes felt different and the touch of our lips caused a wave of excitement and pleasure that traveled up and down and around and through us. And a touch of hand to body was almost more than could be borne, every place touched awakened another place. And through it all,

74

there was a sense of differentness, that we were different than we had been before and that we were different from other people. But there was a sense of sameness, too, a feeling of belonging, of experiencing what someone in a meadow in Asia or on a hill in California might be experiencing and of making contact with everyone else at the very moment that we felt unique and separate. We felt totally come together, with the universe fallen away from us and yet we felt more a part of it than ever before.

The sheer wonder of it simply amazed us, the wonder of the pleasure—we knew that we had never known what pleasure was before—and the awesomeness of the feelings we felt, the deepness of them, the tenderness and the horniness coming all together. To be able to feel deep, deep, tender love and almost unbearable horniness all at the same time was like everything we had ever wished for in the most private recesses of our minds. Finally to come together in ourselves, to bring the two separate halves together and not to feel guilty because it's right and we know it in every fiber and in every secret, terrible part of us. Deeper and deeper we melted into each other and how can you think about a breast and a planet and a universe and all the vibrant life in it at the same time as you are laughing and crying because you never, never knew what love was before, you only had an inkling?

We clung to each other for a long time then, so close, so tight with our tears on her cheeks and our eyes deep into each other and then one of us, I don't remember which, said "So that's what it's all about." And suddenly it was so simple, the meaning of life. The dumb jokes— "Life is like a well,"—and all the wars and the territorial imperative and the Third Reich and Cadillacs and split-level ranchhouses and the Spanish Inquisition and Jesus of Nazareth and Nietzsche and Kant and Marx and all of the madness fell into perspective. We fell asleep holding each other close.

The next morning I was up-tight, irritable, Franklin Pangborn behind the reception desk, suspicious, eyeing the luggage. There was a gulf between us, a feeling of "Don't think you can take advantage." I felt a stiffness in my pelvis like the steel wool had been moved over an inch and then resewn. My eyes were out of focus and things seemed unclear and small affronts bugged me out of proportion.

I had an appointment with Baker and I told him what had happened. He nodded. "That's good," he said. "If you can relax even more the experience will become even deeper. The tendency is to hold the breath and that shuts off the flow of the energy. Holding the breath feels safe and we all tend to do it. Look, you're doing it right now." I realized that I was doing so and I lay there on the bed and tried to relax and breathe easily and tears came to my eyes. "I love her so much," I said, "but I'm so fucking scared." I never really felt right using that word in front of Baker. What a strange complex man he is, I thought, all in a second, that I can lie here in front of him in my terrible jockey shorts and talk about my deepest longings and yell and scream and pound on the bed if I want to but still I feel I should watch my language.

I like him, I decided; forget the crap about analytical transference or my gratitude to him for helping me or anything. I really did like him, even though he was so painfully shy and almost unapproachable that you always wondered if you were out of place to make a word of chit-chat after the session. I had seen him once socially with other of his patients, ex-patients and associates at a party for the publication of his book, and I noticed that I was the only one who called him Elsworth. To everyone else he was Dr. Baker. He seemed to inspire that, even among his peers, and I felt, in a way, that it was a shame. He was like what I imagined Reich must have been with his co-workers, a figure of awe and wonder but lonely and by himself, really.

It had taken me a long time to come to calling him by his first name. But I figure if you almost shit on a guy's bed you can call him Elsworth. Anyway, I liked him. I suppose he must be some kind of genius and I guess they're always alone.

"Yes," he said, "you will be frightened and you will clamp down and feel defensive and angry. You'll move a step forward and then you'll pull back. But just keep at it. You're making progress."

I left his office and went over to Carolyn's place. She was working on a dress for some dreadful lady's teen-aged daughter, making it the way the daughter had wanted it though it was the lady who had the money and wouldn't hire her again. I poured myself a cup of coffee in her closet-kitchen and came out and stood across the room from her.

"All right, what is it?" she said.

"What do you mean?" I said.

"You know," she said.

"Oh Christ," I said, "I guess I'm just scared to death.

77

I never felt so close to anyone in my life. I never felt anything so wonderful and I'm not used to it and it frightens me."

"Well it frightens me too, you know," she said and she stretched out her arms to me and I stepped toward her, only going half way and held out my arms and she laughed and came the rest of the way into my arms and we began to cry and laugh again and I started to feel the waves of tenderness for her. I knew I wanted to marry her then, I knew I had to but I waited to ask her, nervous, a dummy. Instead I sat down, grumbling about some papers I had to have that I had left by mistake out at my little beach cottage in Westhampton, a two-hour drive. I was doing a show every night and a number of other jobs, and I was exhausted and overworked and she said, "Let me drive out to get them for you."

"No," I said, up-tight, feeling like a schmuck for having forgotten the papers, feeling like I couldn't let myself off the hook, I had to be perfect.

"But why?" she asked.

"I left them there, I'll get them," I said, Alan Ladd in *Guns of the Khyber Pass.*

"You never let me do anything for you," she said. She sat there, small, with tears in her eyes and finally, my idiotic New England false pride melted and I knew she really wanted to do it for me.

"O.K." I said.

"Thank you," she said.

"Will you marry me," I said, "because I need you very much."

Her eyes widened. "Do you really mean it?"

I nodded.

"I thought you'd never ask. Can I tell Sheila?" Like that would make it real.

I laughed and said "Sure." We hugged each other and then she called Sheila and I kept hold of her hand while she was on the phone and I felt the soft, melting, streaming sensations again in my pelvis. I thought of something that I had read in one of Reich's books and had subsequently discussed with Baker, that love, the emotion of love, can be felt in the genitals. Not necessarily sexual love, but affection and concern and tenderness can be felt as a stirring in the genitals. I remember feeling it once, sitting in the dressing room of a theater with a friend of mine, an actor of whom I had grown fond, and wondering if I were a fag. Women holding their babies will sometimes feel it and worry that they are developing incestuous desires and shut off the love they feel for the baby. What multiple layers of misunderstandings and what endless tiny tragedies build up because of our ignorance of our sexual nature and our almost pathological fear of finding out about it.

Sheila came home from work with a bottle of California champagne and we all toasted us and we picked a date in October that would give her time to make a dress and me time to stop my heart from pounding and moving up into my throat where it might choke me to death. Then we all three went over to Spark's Pub, where we had met, and then we went down to Edward's to tell Michael McCourt, the bartender, and he was just as happy as we were.

TWELVE

Because the commuting in city traffic from my apartment on the upper east side of Manhattan to The Fifteenth Street School on the lower west side was the equivalent of coming in from Scarsdale, I decided that I might as well live downtown in Greenwich Village. I found two floors of an old house on historic old MacDougal Alley for rent. The master bedroom was immense . . . it could have had goalposts in it. The other two bedrooms, one for Michele and one for Bridie, were Lilliputian. Bridie grumbled more than somewhat, not about the size of her room, but because she felt the move to the Village spelled the end of her social life. Irish-American society centers around East Eighty-sixth Street in Yorkville, near where we had lived for three years. On Thursdays, the Eighty-sixth Street dancehalls are jammed with maids, nannies and elevator operators of Hibernian persuasion.

The huge master bedroom in my new place was absolutely stunning. It had a working fireplace and a curved wall with an enormous window in it which looked out onto trees and carriage houses and when Carolyn and I got married, we decided to do so in that bedroom. We invited fifty people we really liked to the wedding. We threw the bed out the window and had it carted away, having bought a new one which would be delivered the day after the wedding. We set up folding chairs and put tons of flowers in the picture window. We were married by Al Carmines, the assistant pastor of the Judson Memorial Church, and we asked him to incorporate a bit of a Hindu wedding vow we liked in his ceremony, which he did. At a certain point in the proceedings I took Carolyn's hand and said, "I take thy hand in mine, yearning for happiness; I ask thee to live with me as thy husband, till both of us with age grow old." Then Carolyn responded . . . "Let us join together and beget little ones, loving each other, with genial minds and hearts, through a hundred autumns."

We played a rock love song by Petula Clark on the phonograph for our wedding music. Carolyn had made a wedding dress for herself, a bridesmaid's dress for Sheila and a flower girl dress for Michele. Bridie looked beautiful. Dr. Baker and his wife came to the wedding and afterwards all the guests had Chinese food. It was the best wedding I ever attended.

Our honeymoon lasted one day because I had to start rehearsals with a new show the day after the marriage. We checked into the Regency Hotel on Park Avenue for the night and the next morning I was up, pacing around the room, waiting for the waiter to bring up the breakfast and leafing through the Gideon Bible. From years of killing time between shows in cheap hotels on the road, I knew by heart the locations of most of the horny parts of the Old Testament, but the poetry of Genesis was my favorite. The breakfast arrived and Carolyn poured out coffee for two.

"Did you ever stop to think about Adam and Eve?" I said. Carolyn shook her head. "Reich has a fascinating theory about the fall from paradise," I went on. "I've never really understood the theory before but I think I do now. Why the hell were Adam and Eve kicked out of the garden just for eating an apple?"

"I don't know," said Carolyn.

"Well," I said, "the apple tree is referred to as the tree of knowledge . . . but all the way through the Bible, the word knowledge is used in the sense of carnal knowledge, right?"

"Right," said Carolyn. "Shem knew Hephzibah and she did beget Hosephat or somebody."

"Right!" I said. "So the apple, the forbidden fruit, represents sexual intercourse. Now, the serpent who tempted Eve to eat the apple is referred to in the Bible as the most 'subtle' beast in the garden. He was a beautiful creature. The serpent is a snake and the snake is the classic Freudian symbol of the phallus. So, Eve is tempted by the symbol of man's penis, or sexual desire, to partake of the fruit of the tree of knowledge, carnal knowledge, and to induce Adam to do the same."

"Original sin," said Carolyn.

"Right," I said. "So man's fall from grace, which means from the unarmored condition—graceful naturalness,

82

happiness, connection with the universe and with God, stems from a sexual act. The serpent has told Eve . . ." I ran my finger up the page, looking for the line, and found it, "'For God doth know that in the day ye eat thereof, then your eyes shall be opened and ye shall be as gods' . . . get it?"

"No," said Carolyn.

"Look," I said, "through the natural, unarmored sex act, which their innocent carnal knowledge would have been, they would achieve total orgasm and feel at one with the universe, at one with God."

"So why did they put on the fig leaves?"

"Because they couldn't stand the full orgastic convulsion and the orgonotic streamings that it produced. They couldn't stand to be like God. It's the whole story of how man armored himself and of the paradise he lost in the process."

"I see," said Carolyn.

"Then God, which is another way of saying their own true natures, turned on them and made them ashamed of their 'flesh,' which is the armored body: tight, hardened and incapable of the beautiful streamings and of surrender to the orgastic convulsion. They covered their nudity to conceal their shame the way the top layer of false social 'morality' covers people's sadomasochistic secondary sexual strivings.

"God condemned Adam to toil 'by the sweat of thy face'—to work compulsively as opposed to natural, meaningful, rewarding toil. He told Eve that her husband 'shall rule over thee' in all things, which is the beginning of the patriarchal, unnatural relationship between the sexes which stems from armored people's distorted view of their sexual roles, and he told her she would bring forth children 'in sorrow.' The hardened, armored pelvis causes unbearable pain in childbirth."

"Remember the Farnsworth's cat?" said Carolyn. We had watched the pet cat of friends of ours giving birth and had seen ecstasy on her face at the moment of delivery. I nodded and went on with my story.

"The serpent, who was once the most 'subtil' and beautiful thing in the garden, even as unarmored, natural sex is beautiful, was condemned to crawl on the ground for eternity." I looked for the place in the book—"'Upon thy belly shalt thou go and dust shalt thou eat all the days of thy life.' The snake still has traces of beauty. Look at his rhythmic movements, reminiscent of the wavy orgonotic streamings. Look at the brilliant colors of some species. Sex, like the snake, is condemned to wallow in the dust through armoring but it, too, has traces of the old beauty.

"So, the story of the Garden of Eden, if you look at it in terms of symbolism, really is the story of man's fall from grace. If we learn how we left paradise it will teach us the way back to it and if you accept Reich's interpretation of the scriptures, the way back to the garden is through achieving orgastic potency, either as an individual or as a species."

"Well, it's fascinating," said Carolyn, "but I can't believe the men who wrote the Old Testament had any of this in mind."

"No, of course not," I said, "but something down in their unconscious, some deep social memory impelled them

84

to come up with this particular explanation for man's eternal misery. The explanation stayed locked in the fable for centuries and the amazing thing is not so much that no one ever deciphered it before but rather that no one ever even asked the question. No one till Reich ever said, "What was it that Adam and Eve did that was so terrible that it could cause thousands of years of agony for an entire species?' Man will do virtually anything to avoid facing the central issue of our lives, which is that human sexual misery is at the root of all of his other difficulties, social, political and economic. And sexual misery will persist as long as man armors his children and man will armor his children as long as society remains in any of the forms it has taken so far in the history of the so-called civilized world."

We sat in the hotel room there for a little while and then Carolyn said, "Maybe the school will be a beginning."

"Maybe," I said. "It's a drop in the bucket but at least we're doing something. When the kids who go to our school grow up, they'll feel differently about themselves than they would have otherwise."

"It's exciting, isn't it?" said Carolyn and we got up and got dressed and left.

THIRTEEN

September came and The Fifteenth Street School opened for business. On the first day of school, Carolyn and I stood downstairs by the front door and as the parents arrived with their offspring, we met them and told them where their homerooms were. Most of the grown-ups hung around for a while in the teachers' room on the first day and had coffee. Carolyn acted as secretary and ran the office. The four-year-old nursery kids, eight of them, came for three hours in the morning and nine five-year-olds came for three hours in the afternoon. The first grade consisted of eleven children who attended from 9 to 3 and that was our school.

A large chunk of the four-story building sat empty and unused but we planned to add a grade each year so that as the oldest kids moved up, we'd fill in from the bottom. That way, as a new crop of young kids came into the school, the older ones, just by being around, would teach them how we operated. Also, by accepting only little children who hadn't been to school before, we figured we'd be starting with a clean slate in each instance and we wouldn't brave Neill's problem of having to deal with hateful attitudes toward school.

We also tried to avoid accepting kids who were obviously screwed up and antisocial. We didn't have any A. S. Neill on our staff and we didn't want to become a therapeutic institution. Carolyn and I had thought a lot about it and what we really wanted was to provide a place where those few people who were trying to raise their kids to be as self-regulated as possible could send them to be educated without lousing up everything they were able to do at home.

On that first day, while the parents sat in the teachers' room, drinking coffee and making small talk, the children checked out their school. The younger ones stayed pretty much under the protective wing of Renee, their teacher, but the older ones, when they heard that they had the freedom of the building, banded together in small groups and flew around the place, examining every cranny and crevice from the roof to the basement. Hours went by. The noise level was incredible and you could almost feel the energy that was being generated. The teachers spent the day racing around after the children, trying to make sure they didn't kill themselves. When three o'clock came and the last of the kids had left, Carolyn and I sat down in the office and looked at each other, wondering what the hell we had started. The teachers wandered in, one by one, exhausted, and sat down and looked at us, too. Carolyn opened the drawer of her desk and pulled out a little jug of Hennessy brandy she had had the foresight to buy and we all poured it into our coffee and drank it.

"What do you think?" said Wilbur.

"I dunno," I said and stared into my coffee. I had hired an out-of-work actor named Ralph to be our janitor. He came into the office looking for a pushbroom and started talking about Chekhov, which drove everybody out of the room, so we all went home and went to bed early.

The second day of school picked up where the first one had left off. It was bedlam. The teachers got through the day somehow and then they flopped down on the couch in the office, exhausted. Days went by. An attempt was made each morning to organize a reading class. Wilbur would stand up at ten o'clock in his homeroom and look around. Four kids with a deck of cards would be sitting on the floor playing Old Maid. A couple more would be sprawled under a table reading comic books. A few would be drawing or painting with water colors. Arnold, our genius, was at a table reading the World Book Encyclopedia. Fat Harry was finishing up his lunch. Wilbur would yell, "Reading class!" The kids would laugh hideously and run out of the room. Only Arnold, the genius, would be left. "Reading class?" Wilbur would ask, plaintively. "No thanks," Arnold would say. "I can already read." When the kids left Wilbur's room, some of them would head upstairs to the empty rooms of the fourth floor. A few would crawl under the stairwell to hide and the rest would head downstairs to the "gym." The "gym" was the large room about 25 by 60 on the ground floor which the old union had used as an auditorium. There wasn't much in it except a large wooden closet-like structure that could be hidden in and a few things to climb on, but it turned out to be the most popular place in the school because there usually weren't any grown-ups in it.

One day about two months into the run, Wilbur announced that it was time for reading class and, to his delight, a few kids stayed in the room. They were joined, the next day, by a few more and before long most of the kids were attending class regularly. By Christmas, there was a vigorous math class going each day, too.

As the first year went on, a pattern of behavior began to emerge with our first grade children. They would arrive at 8:30 or 9 A.M., most of them having ridden to school from various parts of Manhattan on the school bus (operated by a private company). They would check into their homerooms, drop off their lunchboxes and race down to the gym to run around and let off steam. At 9:15 or so, Wilbur and Rachel would each announce reading class and the group would subdivide into two smaller groups, with the exception of Arnold, who, at the age of six, already read better than Wilbur, and two other boys, Anthony and Danny, who couldn't read at all and didn't care. The session lasted about an hour and the level of concentration during that time was extraordinarily high. The rule was that anyone who didn't want to take class could stay in the room if he were absolutely quiet (Arnold) or leave and go elsewhere if he had to be noisy (Anthony and Danny). The rule was enforced with no difficulty. It's one thing to insist that a kid sit still and pay attention to a reading class (as most schools do) and another thing to insist that he choose between the options of sitting still and paying attention to a reading class or leaving the room and doing something else. When children are given this kind of a choice, respectful attention can be demanded by the teachers as a matter of course, if the child decides to stay and participate. Reading class was over at 10:15 or 10:30 and then the children turned to things like arts and crafts, which Rachel handled, or racing around in the gym, or going up to the playroof (fenced in, tiled, and stocked with a certain amount of outdoor play equipment), or bugging Wilbur to help them with science experiments (boys), or goofing off under the stairwell with a comic book or wandering the halls aimlessly (Anthony and Danny). The kids ate their lunch at about 11:30 except for Fat Harry, who had always opened and consumed his by 10 in the morning. Lunches were eaten all over the building in groups of twos, threes and fours. Wilbur complained continuously about lunch—garbage being left in the gym for him to clean up at the end of the day. He called several meetings about it and encountered nothing but lethargy. Finally, he railroaded through a resolution that lunch not be eaten in the gym anymore. The ruling was observed intermittently. After lunch came math class. Fewer kids elected to attend math than reading but the course was taught, anyway, for those who wanted it. The last hour or so of the day was devoted to finishing off projects, cleaning up, racing around in the gym or wandering the halls aimlessly. Sprinkled throughout the week were such activities as trips away from school to zoos, museums, parks, the garment center, pet stores, China-town, the Staten Island ferry, exhibits, the Empire State Building and anything of interest around New York City

90

that the teachers would think of. Wilbur believed, and I agree with him, that a large percentage of the meaningful learning experiences in a kid's life take place underground — that is, after school and away from the home. Children's play, organized by themselves and utilizing the things around them (cheap plastic toys, Coke bottles, fire escapes, etc.), involves counting, reasoning, calculating and interpersonal development. It's a lot more rewarding, meaningful and important than 95 percent of what goes on in the classroom. We decided to try to incorporate as much as we could of this play into the school day. We encouraged the children to bring their dreadful (to us) plastic toys to school. We didn't merely tolerate what seemed to us to be aimless play, or "goofing off," we affirmed a kid's right to it and we tried to see in it the importance that the kid attached to it. Gradually, it dawned on me to what an extent we grown-ups are prejudiced against children's interests and desires. Children's literature, for instance, is always supposed to be uplifting. The same people who read Jacqueline Susann, because her stuff gives them pleasure, wouldn't dream of buying a book for their kids that wasn't edifying, instructive and nonviolent. But their children are just as interested in pleasure as they are. The whole field of children's literature is a little like the cat food business. The purchaser and the consumer are not one and the same. The cat food has to taste fishy enough to appeal to the cat but not smell fishy enough to drive the housewife who has the money to buy it out of the kitchen.

At The Fifteenth Street School we saw that children learn through what seemed to us to be aimless play, which means that it isn't aimless at all. But we never went the route of trying to trick a kid into learning something we wanted him to learn by disguising it as play. Any kid worth his salt hates those "learning can be fun" magazines you see in the children's doctors' offices. He'll choose *Archie Comics* anytime.

By the end of our first year, all of the children in the first grade except Arnold, Anthony and Danny were coming regularly to classes in reading, writing and math. In February and March of that year, we had interviewed and accepted a new group of four-year-old nursery kids for the following September and we had added a few more in kindergarten and first grade. The first graders would now move up to become our second grade, the kindergarten would graduate to first grade, etc. When we reopened the following September, to our delight, all the children who had gotten into the habit of regular attendance at class picked up exactly where they had left off the previous June and we knew we were in business as a school.

FOURTEEN

One year and ten days after our wedding, Max Bean was born at the Beth Israel Hospital in New York City. He was supposed to have been born at home on MacDougal Alley in the bedroom where his mother and father were married and where he was conceived. Carolyn has never felt that a kid should start out life in a hospital and she so convinced her obstetrician, a wonderful old European who said he had delivered hundreds of babies at home before everything got so fancy. His only reason for hesitating was the fact that if his fellow doctors had heard that he had agreed to a home delivery, they'd think he was crazy. In any event, he did agree with the stipulation that we hire a nurse-midwife to assist him. We found one, a charming and efficient former head nurse from the New York Hospital, who lived in New Jersey but could be at MacDougal Alley within the hour when contractions began. Her name was Betty Hosford and she had had her

93

own children at home. Carolyn and I attended Mrs. Bing's classes in natural childbirth for young expectant couples. The other husbands and I dutifully learned all the breathing exercises so that if our wives forgot to do them in the course of their labor we would be able to remind them when to inhale or exhale. The day arrived, the contractions began, Mrs. Hosford started in from New Jersey and the doctor told us to keep him informed by phone as to how his patient was progressing. Carolyn sat in our king-sized bed in her most beautiful nightgown, looking absolutely radiant. Michele perched on the edge of the bed and watched fascinated, as we did our breathing exercises when the contractions came. I made a daiquiri on the rocks for the mother-to-be (the doctor had said there was no harm in a little drink, as it only tended to relax people), Michele turned on the television, the nurse-midwife arrived, the contractions started to get closer together, I called the doctor, he came to MacDougal Alley and Max Bean prepared to enter into his own home.

Except that he never dropped. The contractions got to be three minutes apart and then a minute apart. Hours went by and then more hours, and the contractions were five minutes apart again and then ten. The doctor called a specialist friend of his who came to our house, examined Carolyn and pronounced her undeliverable. He said, "Get her to the hospital and perform a Caesarean." Our man was stubborn: She would be delivered naturally. Carolyn had been in labor now for thirty-six hours! The idyllic home delivery turned into a nightmare. We bundled her into our car and took her to Beth Israel Hospital, where we had made a provisional reservation in case of

94

emergency. They were wonderful. A team of doctors hovered over Carolyn. The baby was lying crosswise and facing the wrong way. To a man they recommended Caesarean. Our old European was adamant. Carolyn was weak and exhausted now and I was frantic. I demanded that our man give in to the wishes of the majority. He said that if she did not deliver in the next two hours he would do so. She was given a medication to induce labor and with about ten minutes to spare, the baby's head appeared. He was delivered with the help of forceps and Carolyn, awake and helping throughout, except for the actual moment of birth, fell into an exhausted sleep. Max was wheeled by me on his way into the nursery and I looked down at him. His fists were tightly clenched and he had deep furrows of worry on his little brow. Small wonder after what he had been through.

I drove up to Dick Edward's bar and ordered a Scotch but I couldn't drink it. I went home and fell asleep in the rumpled bed which should have contained my wife and son. All was well, but what a shame that with all the women in the world who would prefer to go to the hospital, get knocked out and be told about it when it's over, Carolyn, who had gone to the time and trouble to prepare this romantic and loving coming out party for her child, should have had complications which prevented it.

The next day, bright and early, I went over to Beth Israel. Carolyn looked more beautiful than I had ever seen her. Her face was scrubbed and her hair pulled back and Max was nursing at her breast. I had on a surgical mask and gown and I sat down on the edge of the bed and she handed him to me. He looked up at me (Wilhelm

Reich has observed that babies' eyes do focus at birth, popular legend to the contrary, if they haven't had painful drops put in them and Max's hadn't, by agreement with the doctor). He still had the deep worry-furrows on his brow and his eyes looked anxious. I handed him back to his mother and he clutched at her breast eagerly. His little hands dug into her skin and he sucked at her like a tiger. I saw him look up at her. She gazed down at him with such love and tenderness that when their eyes met they seemed to melt into one being. My vision blurred and I felt overwhelmed with love for the two of them.

It was time for Max to go back to his nursery. I followed him out of the room and down the hall as the nurse wheeled him away in his bassinette. He disappeared into a door and reappeared behind a large glass window with a dozen other babies. I stood in front of it watching him, when I was joined by an old Jewish grandfather wearing a hat.

"That's my grandson," he said proudly, pointing to a pale-faced baby two cribs over from Max.

"Nice looking kid," I said. "That's my son there." I indicated Max's bassinette.

"A nice looking boy," said the old man. "What's his name?"

"Max," I said.

"Max!" he exclaimed and began to wave his arms around in excitement. "Max! Max! What a great old name," said the old Jewish grandfather. "Why don't they name the kids the great old names anymore! Me? I'm surrounded by Geoffries!"

Carolyn, having gone through as difficult a delivery

96

as could be wished on anyone the day before, was now begging to be allowed to take her son and go home. The doctor said that if she felt all right on the third day she could leave. The hospital staff, realizing that time was short, set about trying to convince the parents of the child born on their premises to do right by it. One after another, the nurses and doctors of this modern, enlightened up-to-date hospital came into Carolyn's room, smiled at her, inquired as to how she felt and then asked why the baby had not been put down for a circumcision. Carolyn explained that the baby's father was not circumcized, that she was aware of all the arguments in favor of it and knew that most people believed in it these days, but that she simply preferred not to have it done.

"But aren't you aware that there is a higher incidence of cancer of the penis among noncircumcized men than circumsized ones?" the staff people would say.

"The statistics are questionable," she would answer, "but if it is true, it probably has to do with lack of cleanliness and we have indoor plumbing and don't expect that to be a problem."

"Well," said one daring nurse, looking around to make sure no one was listening, "there is the question of sexual prowess. It's well known that circumcized men have greater staying power than uncircumcized men." She smiled knowingly at Carolyn, who resisted the temptation to ask her how extensively she had researched the point herself. Instead she replied, "My husband isn't circumcized and I have no complaints."

"Well, you don't know what you're missing," said the nurse. When the staff realized that reason was not going

97

to prevail, they became increasingly insistent and almost hostile, issuing implicit warnings that we would live to regret our actions. The obvious depth of feeling on the subject startled me. Nature's purpose in creating the foreskin is to protect the sensitive head of the penis so that it will be capable of providing as much pleasure as possible to its owner. If the foreskin is removed, the sensitive head of the penis, exposed over the years to jockey shorts and preshrunk no-iron corduroy pants, will toughen up and be less sensitive. In a culture oriented to "successful performance" of the sex act this may seem an asset. Basically, it represents an antipleasure attitude, despite all the spurious health claims which are used to cover this up. Orgonomists know that the act of circumcision is a terror-filled trauma for a baby; they see the results of it in their patients' unconscious. The myth that a newborn baby's nervous system is not yet developed to the point where he feels much pain is one of the fallacies that people have from time to time found convenient to believe, such as: "Children have no sexual feelings," "Negroes have no souls" and "The earth is at the center of the universe."

On the afternoon of Carolyn's second day in the hospital, a nurse came into her room to demonstrate how the baby should be wrapped in its blankets. "Wrap them tightly," she said. "It gives them a feeling of security. They may cry at first but stick it out. They really do prefer it, even in the hottest of weather." Max Bean, aged two days, lay loosely wrapped in his mother's arms, listening to this, kicking his feet and waving his arms. The concept of swaddling clothes seems to have its origins in the same antipleasure, antilife, antifreedom-of-movement feelings as circumcision.

On the third day, I went to pick up Carolyn and Max and bring them home. I had put fresh flowers in the bedroom and Michele had helped make the bed and straighten up the room. I stood in line at the hospital cashier's window to pay the bill, which turned out to be remarkably modest, incidentally, considering the superb medical attention they had given Carolyn. The cashier checked over my account and said, "There doesn't seem to be a charge on here for circumcision."

"There wasn't any," I mumbled.

"What?" asked the cashier incredulously.

"There was no circumcision," I said, as quietly as possible.

"No circumcision!" The waiter's voice resounded through the hall, we don't serve bread with one fish ball. I could hear an angry murmuring growing in the line behind me. Before the mob could be galvanized into action, I gave the cashier the money, gathered up my brood and beat a retreat to MacDougal Alley.

Every day the furrow on Max's brow lessened and by the time he was two weeks old it had gone away entirely. His little fists unclenched and as he partook of Carolyn's seemingly endless supply of milk (delicious, I might add), mother and child would gaze into each other's eyes and father would melt with happiness. The traumatic birth was forgotten and Max Bean set about the business of exploring his world, which was, for the moment, a closet-sized alcove off the bedroom where his parents were married on MacDougal Alley.

99

FIFTEEN

The last time I went to see Dr. Baker professionally was shortly after Max was born. The therapy had lasted approximately three and a half years, once a week for the first three years and a decreasing number of times after that. My psychoanalysis had lasted ten years at three times a week. I once asked Baker if he felt that the fact that I had been psychoanalyzed had helped or hindered my treatment in orgonomy and he replied that he didn't think it had mattered one way or the other. Looking back, I tend to agree; the two experiences had very little to do with each other. In psychoanalysis it seemed that I talked endlessly about my feelings but I almost never felt them. If I felt like crying, I said so but I never cried. If I felt furious, I told the analyst so but my expressions of rage consisted of raising my voice slightly once in a while. Lying on a couch with one's back to the analyst, in classic Freudian style, is supposed to keep the doctor from getting

100

involved with the patient and it does. In orgonomy, the patient does get involved with the doctor although the doctor retains professional control over the relationship. I felt as frustrated for ten years trying to make contact with my psychoanalyst as I had felt as a child trying to make contact with my parents.

If you ask a psychiatrist what mental health consists of and what he hopes to achieve when he treats his patients he will answer, if he is candid, that there are no absolute standards of mental health and that he feels the analysis has been successful if the patient finishes it happier than when he went in and better able to adjust to society and to his life. The orgonomist has specific goals in sight when he takes on a patient. To the extent that he is able to help his patient achieve these goals, the ultimate of which is orgastic potency, he knows he has succeeded. He knows that true health can exist only where orgastic potency has been established and can be maintained. He knows that practically everything in society works against these ends and that orgonomy is no cure-all and that not all patients can be helped, much less brought to orgastic potency.

The changes I underwent in my three and a half years in orgonomy were profound. As I grew more and more "natural" I began to see things around me quite differently. The meaning of sex and love became clearer to me and I came to understand that the people who claim that they represent two different drives in man are influenced to see things this way by their armoring.

Sexually, I found myself able to tolerate more and more pleasure, without clamping down in anxiety, and I found

101

that the sexual pleasure I experienced was increasingly intertwined with my soft, tender feelings. I felt infinitely freer sexually than ever before, but it had nothing to do with the so-called sexual revolution which has produced a phenomenon Reich called "freedom peddlers."

"Freedom peddlers" go around tantalizing and titillating people with sugarplum visions of the new world they claim we are about to enter. They advocate immediate sexual freedom without ever taking into consideration the fact that the people in this world are sex-starved and have been for centuries. It's ignorant and irresponsible to offer a starving man a full-course dinner; he has to start out with broth. The human race will have to rise up out of its sexual abyss slowly and carefully like a deep-sea diver trying to avoid the bends.

Centuries ago, great men like Moses came up with elaborate plans for coping with people's sex-starved natures. The Ten Commandments were necessary because Moses saw that the Hebrews couldn't handle freedom in a self-regulated way. If somebody gave them a table of food they wouldn't eat what they needed and leave the rest for someone else, they'd gorge themselves until they got sick and threw up. When they felt the stir of love, they wouldn't look for a mate to tenderly embrace, they'd have an orgy and wring themselves sexually dry until they were filled with self-loathing. The Chosen People were rapidly going down the drain until Moses saw that they needed what all other undisciplined children, Hebrew or otherwise, need: external regulation. He used every weapon at his command to whip them into line, appealing to their superstition, fear, guilt and anxiety. They were

102

so out of touch with their own instincts that they couldn't tell the difference between right and wrong so he arbitrarily made up a bunch of "shalt nots" and saved their necks in the process. They've worshiped him ever since.

Thousands of years later, we see that Moses' "shalt nots" are arbitrary and we start to reject them. But we're no more capable of self-regulation now than the Israelites were then. The heralded new sexual freedom produces *Screw Magazine* and *Spankers Monthly* and executive wife-swapping.

I wasn't brought up in the Trobriand Islands and I'm not knocking dirty pictures. What I'm saying is that if we listen to the "freedom peddlers," who don't give a damn about us, and if we move too quickly toward an ideal, however desirable it may be in theory, we're going to get the bends. Then we'll feel like the Hebrew children. We'll start looking around for a savior and there's already more than one would-be Moses warming up in the bullrushes.

Dr. Baker had told me, and it turned out to be true, that when a patient finishes orgone therapy, the capacity to change which has been established in him will continue and he can find himself to be quite different a year after the completion of the treatment than he was when he finished it. One way in which I changed was that I became less able to tolerate the filth and degradation of life in New York City, feeling an almost physical oppression radiating from the squalid surroundings and the angry, frustrated people.

My perception of politics changed too. I listened to the extreme new-left in this country: the Yippies and the Crazies and the Weathermen. They believe that America

103

is covertly fascist and that as long as our system of life and government remains in its present form, or anything like it, there is no hope for happiness for the people. They're not interested in reform. On the contrary, they know that reform is the enemy of revolution and that anything that helps to make our system more acceptable to the people will perpetuate it and postpone the eventual revolution.

It's true that our system is an authoritarian one, however benevolent. It is based on the partriarchal family unit, on male superiority over females, on suppression of infant and adolescent sexuality, on a basically repressive and Victorian school system which attempts to break a child's spirit and on a compulsive, consumer-oriented economy which requires the endless wasteful production of goods with built-in obsolescence. The revolutionary kids see this vision of Amerika much more clearly than anyone else does.

The difference, according to the revolutionary kids, between our society and Hitler's is our thin veneer of pseudo-freedom which cynically slicks over what we really are. It's their plan to strip this veneer away by confrontation. By painting their faces, lengthening their hair, wearing socially unacceptable clothes and deliberately carrying on contemptuously, like spoiled brats, they hope to so infuriate the establishment that it will drop its pretenses of benevolence and be exposed as brutish and dictatorial. When liberal sympathizers complain that they could basically support the changes these kids want to bring about "if only they didn't look and act so far-out and crazy," they are missing the whole point and they earn the contempt the revolutionaries heap on them. The kids consider the liberals the most dangerous part of the establishment because the reforms they press for tend to perpetuate what the revolution sees as the myth of democracy.

When the revolution strikes, it will have no chance of winning and it knows this. But it will accomplish its true aim of bringing the fascists out of the woodwork and making the people choose sides. When a junta runs the country and stormtroopers come in the night to take suspects away, the decent, caring people will have no place to go but underground. A romantic popular revolution will build up with the "best" people involved in it. Acts of sabotage on the part of the underground will be met by acts of retaliation on the part of the establishment. Life for Americans will become a question of either/or and the social veneer of democracy will be a thing of the past. Freedom will consist of joining the revolution. What the eventual outcome will be no one knows, but the kids have decided it's worth the chance because they figure anything is better than continuing the centuries-old pattern of war and misery and lifelong compulsive monogamy and Keeping Up With The Joneses and lives devoted to the acquisition of material possessions.

The tragedy of the revolutionary kids is that they yearn for freedom but they don't know that any attempt to bring *genuine* freedom to the armored millions of the world will be fought tooth and nail by the millions themselves. The hallmark of the armored person is that he cannot tolerate expansive movement or true freedom, except in extremely limited amounts. He has never been or wanted to be his own boss, settling instead for a periodic change of masters.

The peasant living in a commune in China has no more or less individual freedom in his life than he would have had in the days of the Ming Dynasty. He may have more food and warmer clothes and it can be argued that this in itself is a freedom, but is that really what the kids in this country are talking about? Obviously, in this land of affluence, not.

What they're pushing for is a society which affirms freedom of the spirit, a society which makes provisions for love and tenderness and communication with nature, a society which, like the Trobriand Islands, truly allows people to do their own thing. What the kids, in their desperation, can't face is that life-affirmative societies evolve out of generations of life-affirmative people. A loving way of life can't be thrust in a revolutionary manner upon people who are basically life-negative. If this is done, the way of life will always revert to negativism, usually in a more virulent form than the revolution had sought to escape (Marx to Stalin, etc.).

The revolutionary kids see this country with great clarity . . . but they are seeing it with armored eyes. The fact of the matter is that while America, like the rest of the western world, is basically authoritarian, it is far from totalitarian. The American revolutionaries have never lived under dictatorship — of the proletariat or otherwise — and they don't have the remotest clue as to what it's like. They fail to see that the first thing that a society does when it goes socialist is to become sexually repressive. This happened in Russia, China, Albania, North Vietnam and Cuba, which today are the most puritanical countries on earth.

106

Most of what the kids say about the country is true but there's a larger truth, which is that the human race, as represented in America, is far from capable of tolerating more freedom than it now enjoys here. In fact, it seems to have difficulty tolerating as much as it has. The thin veneer of freedom which exists in America is, unfortunately, all that the vast majority of human beings can handle. More freedom than this, which would require us to take more responsibility for our own destinies, would make nervous wrecks out of us and we would reject it. The tragic mistake that the kids make in not understanding this, which, of course, they can't possibly do, is to drive us toward a loss of the freedom we *do* have.

The slow ascent toward freedom which has taken thousands of years to reach its present level here in the United States is about to be reversed, ironically, by the clearest thinkers that the freest society in history has yet produced. It's no good to think clearly if you're armored—your thinking will turn inside out. The fuzzy-headed conservative, who thinks with his heart and loves his country, winds up closer to the real truth about America and the human condition than the incredibly lucid young revolutionary who seems to see us as we really are.

What's happening with this mock-revolution terrifies me. It's a prison break, ill-planned, doomed to failure and steam-rollering out of control. My experience with orgonomy has made me see it differently than most people—I think, more clearly. It hasn't made me like it.

SIXTEEN

Bridie survived the trip from Eighty-sixth Street to Washington Square. It took her about a day to accustom herself to the smell of pot and the sight of interracial couples and after that she never looked at another elevator operator. After Carolyn and I were married, though, she began to feel like a fifth wheel and one day she announced that she was going back to Ireland. Her hometown was Dingle and she married a young man in it and settled down and had a baby. Max and Michele had a little sister named Susannah and we bought a house, an old rooming house which we renovated, on the same block as the school.

The school grew and expanded until it had a hundred kids in it and it went up through the sixth grade. All but six of the original children who had started with it drifted away. Fat Harry's parents moved to the suburbs, taking Fat Harry with them. Arnold the genius went, after one year with us, to a school for geniuses. Danny's parents put him in public school after four years. Anthony was still around. After a year and a half or so of wandering the halls, he had become bored, looked in on a reading class and gotten hooked.

We tried to follow up on as many of the children as we could who had left us after spending one, two or three years at our school and then gone on to more traditional schools. We wanted to find out how well they had made the transition. Most of their families had left New York City in the great middle-class exodus, but the ones we could contact reported that their children seem to have had no trouble in their new school experiences. Two sisters, Tracy and Lisa Ticknor, moved with their parents to upstate New York and went to the local public school in their town. Tracy had sobbed bitterly at first but Lisa found that she preferred sitting at a desk all day. "This," she said, "is what school is supposed to be." Both girls did fine. None of the children who left the school apparently found the transition particularly difficult. Liz Kamell, who stayed with us for the first five years we were open before her parents were forced out of the city by high rents, lack of suitable living space and twenty-five dollar parking tickets, missed the Fifteenth Street School terribly. But one of the things that Liz was, because of the way she had been brought up and educated, was reasonable. She accepted her new school with its more structured set-up because she had to, and she appears to be doing fine in it.

We acquired a full-time director, Patty Greene, who had been one of our teachers. We learned from our mistakes, we accumulated a larger and an exceptional staff. We renovated the building as we used more of it and we

109

became, by our own standards, the most successful school around. The students developed a sense of morality, decency and fair-play that was remarkable and touching. No matter how many times I walked into the building I was struck by how different our children were from the children in any other school. When I conducted visitors through the place I had an opportunity to see it through their eyes and I was always proud of the kids. They had, without being preached at, learned the lesson that maximum personal freedom (which means minimal government) requires maximum personal responsibility. The few kids who, over the years, elected not to attend classes knew this just as well as the vast majority who attended classes regularly. There was never a sense of frivolity or promiscuity in the school even though there was lots of laughter. No kid, enrolled in a reading class, would have dreamed of showing up at it on Monday and Tuesday, staying away on Wednesday and returning on Thursday. Either he was in the class or he wasn't. Anything else would have been disrespectful to the teacher and to the other children in the class.

We started giving the Stanford Achievement Test to the students at the end of each year and we found, to our delight, that the overwhelming majority of them scored in the upper nineties, not surprising for a small private school, but remarkable if you consider the fact that attendance at class was voluntary. The school grew and thrived and even became economically independent, helped out by a few parents like Charles and Jane Prussack, who not only sent us four great kids, but offered a healthy financial assist. By minimizing our administrative expenses, we were able to keep tuitions down and could still pay our teachers better than most other private schools in New York do.

We even were visited by A. S. Neill. I had been scheduled to guest-host the *Tonight Show* for N.B.C. Carolyn said to me, "Why don't you see if they'd be willing to fly Neill over? What a great guest he'd make."

"He'd never do it," I said. "He hasn't been in America in twenty years."

"Well," she said, "what have you got to lose?"

I asked N.B.C. and they agreed. I placed a trans-Atlantic phonecall to Summerhill. Neill's wife, Ena, answered. "It's a grand idea," she said. "It will do the old man good. He's down at the tobacco shop in Leiston now. When he comes back, I'll talk him into it."

To everyone's surprise and delight, three days later A. S. Neill was in New York for a week's stay. He lived at our house, visited with his publisher and with old friends he had never expected to see again and he was the best guest the *Tonight Show* ever had. He went up to Connecticut to see Reich's widow, Ilse. He talked with our students ("I like their faces," he said) and he spoke to a hundred people or so who crowded into our school gymnasium and contributed ten dollars each to the Summerhill Building Fund.

But the best thing, for us, was the evenings he spent, sitting with me and Carolyn on the comfortable sofa in our living room. I had opened a jug of twenty-five-year-old Chivas Regal scotch which some advertising agency had given me for Christmas and Neill and I got into it at some length and we all talked. I asked him about Reich.

"God, he was a pigheaded man," he said. "When some plague-ridden journalist or other would attack him, he'd sit down and write endless letters to the editor defending himself. I'd say, 'Forget them, Reich, have a drink.' But he never could. He really liked me and he knew I really liked him. I think he went off the deep end a bit toward the last of it, seeing flying saucers and all and spies in the government. Oh, he was a great genius all right, although I never could understand all that stuff about the cosmic orgone energy. I had an accumulator in my room for years, but I never knew for sure if it did any good. He was right about people and their sex lives, though. Poor old Reich, I remember him sitting there, chain smoking and talking to me. Sometimes I think I was the only one he could talk to, the rest of them worshiped him so."

A few minutes with A. S. Neill was all it took to know you were in the presence of one of the warmest and wisest men in the world. Carolyn and I visited him and Ena subsequently at Summerhill, when I was in England making a movie. She is as wonderful as he.

Every other day, it seems, I hear a rumor that Neill is dead and Summerhill closed. I hear the same rumors about our school; either the state has closed it or else it has changed and no longer practices "freedom without license." These rumors seem to be the work of what Reich called the "emotional plague." The unique and special properties of the "emotional plague" as opposed to any other form of destructive behavior is that the individuals under its influence attack people who seemingly pose no threat to them. "Plague" individuals are usually energetic, attractive, intelligent and active. They have a high energy content but they are incapable of achieving release of this energy through pleasurable sex. When they come in contact with healthy, loving life, maybe in the form of an ebullient and happy child or a young couple glowingly in love or even a scientist involved in his work to the exclusion of all else, the sheer life-force generated by these healthy, functioning people excites the high energy content of the "plague" individual the way one magnetic force excites another. But the energy, once excited, can't get out because of the sexual hang-up. This creates incredible frustration and a murderous rage, which turns on the object that caused the excitation. When the armored crowd demanded that Barabbas' life be spared instead of Jesus', it was an example of the "emotional plague" at work.

At The Fifteenth Street School, we've had a few examples of "plague" behavior. The attractive mother of an adorable child who had been in the school for three years, obviously having a wonderful time learning, laughing and loving every minute of it, came to me one day and said, most pleasantly, that some of the parents seemed to have complaints and suggestions and that they didn't know how to go about communicating them. Wouldn't it be a good idea, she wondered, if there were some kind of a parent board through which suggestions and criticisms could be channeled? It sounded like a good plan to me and I asked her if she would help to organize it. "Well, if you want me to," she said. The board was organized in a week and immediately there was an outpouring of vicious, hostile, personal invective directed against some of the teachers. When it was traced down, it turned out to have come from only three or four people but under the school-sanctioned mantle of the parent suggestion board. It was blown up out of proportion and caused a great deal of concern and some

113

bitterness. A week after the initial outpouring of venom, the young mother casually mentioned that she was really too busy to serve on the parent board and that that sort of thing bored her anyway. A few weeks after that, we received word that her child had been enrolled for the following year in another school. Only gradually did the whole picture become clear to me. Why on earth, I asked myself, did this woman, who had never seemed to be anything but the school's biggest supporter, bother to whip up this hornets' nest and then move out? The only answer I could come up with was that the sight of her own child, blossoming and growing and glowing, simply became too much for her. However she may have wanted it for her child on an intellectual level (she often mentioned how she had hated school as a kid and how she envied the experience her child was having), it apparently caused an excitement in her which finally became unbearable.

The bit of mischief this woman helped cause is, of course, a very minor example of "emotional plague" behavior, but a clear-cut one. (Incidentally, some valuable suggestions came out of the parent board along with the destructive ones.) The "plague" killed Reich by the use of slander, abuse and lies, which drove him from country to country, made it next to impossible for him to do his work and finally put him in prison, where he died.

The Fifteenth Street School will, hopefully, survive the vicissitudes of the "emotional plague" and other disasters, natural and unnatural. The kids in it are thriving, the building is alive and the front door is still painted bright yellow.

114

SEVENTEEN

On a balmy Sunday afternoon Carolyn and I walked over to Washington Square. The young kids were sitting around the fountain strumming their guitars and singing protest songs. The sweet smell of pot hung over the area so strongly that it seemed as if the cops walking past could get high just by breathing deeply. We walked in silence, holding hands, both of us thinking about these kids around the fountain and the world they'd come into, and which they're obviously out to change.

They really think they're healthier than the generation that spawned them or, for that matter, any other generation. In fact, they seem to be convinced that they are almost a different species and that they are capable of a new way of life and can somehow produce a happier and more loving society.

It's obvious to anyone who spends any amount of time with these kids that the basis for the feeling of "differentness" on their part is not political but sexual. They believe that they are the first sexually free generation in history. They feel sexually free, at least relatively; they feel capable of loving and capable of sustaining a society based on love.

"They really do feel different," I said to Carolyn as we strolled past the fountain that day, "and do you know what I think the reason may be? Pot."

"Maybe so," she said and we walked on, thinking about it. There's no doubt that this is the turned-on generation. They are smoking pot in unheard-of amounts and pot is an aphrodisiac. LSD is an aphrodisiac, too, and that's the other big drug the kids are flirting with. The feeling you get from smoking good pot is remarkably similar to the feeling produced by the orgonotic streamings. The sexual act, under the influence of good pot, is an unbelievably wonderful, never-to-be-forgotten experience. With all of the bushels of words that have been turned out about pot and LSD, relatively little has been said about the sheer fun involved. But that's what's driving the kids to use it and this has to be faced. I have a hunch that what pot does is to temporarily break down the armoring and allow the orgone energy to stream through the body. A stick of really good pot causes waves of pleasure to start at the toes and move up through the body to the top of the head again and again. It's an experience of such pure pleasure that it's difficult to describe. (Most pot doesn't produce quite this experience and one of the problems resulting from its being illegal is lack of quality control.) Having sex with a compatible partner while under the influence of pot can produce a feeling that one is bursting with love

116

and this makes one desire to change the world in order to share this love. I'd never dare to try LSD but I'm told that the experience can be even more so. I wonder if the kids aren't temporarily de-armoring themselves by mechanical means and when they do, they look at this armored society and they simply can't stand it. It's possible that the so-called bad trip on LSD occurs because the user can't bear the sudden de-armoring and feels as though he is going to fly apart at the seams and joints. But kids are willing to risk anything to feel alive and free and like part of the universe. The reason they know the old folks will never understand them is that they know the old folks aren't turning on.

The problem is, of course, that you can't stay high all the time and when you come down your armoring returns and you are reminded that you are your parents' child and you hate them and yourself and your society and you lash out. You'll do *anything* to get back to where you were because it really is a better feeling. But everything has its price and that includes pot, although we don't really know what that price is yet. LSD has its price too and now we have the horror of kids moving on to heroin. We can't achieve freedom through drugs because there's a law of diminishing returns in their use and because a whole society can't walk around stoned out of its skull all the time no matter what the kids say. The Cotton Mathers of this country who hate pleasure are just biding their time waiting to pounce and, given the inevitable futility of the drug thing, in a terrible way they are right. When the antipleasure crowd strikes, there'll be no more pot and no more LSD and a lot less fucking and we'll be right back where armored people belong — in the miserable trap we created for ourselves out of our own fear of love and nature.

The trap is man's armored character structure and there's only one way out of it. It's not drugs and it's not religion and it's not politics. It's going back to the old apple tree and trying to do better than Adam and Eve did. It's trying to raise our kids to be more loving (most of the people who try won't understand how and will produce spoiled brats) and trying to learn to tolerate what little bits of love we see in human behavior and nurturing those bits in hopes that they'll blossom and spread. We mustn't delude ourselves that any kind of a revolution can work nor must we despair that slow progress isn't fast enough. It *is* fast enough because it's all we can stand and if we try to move faster we'll wind up three paces back.

Carolyn and I walked away from the fountain and the guitar music and the kids and headed back toward Fifteenth Street. At a point in time when our country and most of the world seem almost psychopathically confused, we feel lucid. We know what we want and we know what our limitations are. We'll go where we have to go and do what we have to do to make a life for ourselves. We walked up Greenwich Avenue past weekend hippies who would soon take the BMT home to Queens and I thought about Wilhelm Reich, whom I had never met, and A. S. Neill, who is my friend, and Elsworth Baker. I thought about the kids who have come and gone in and out of The Fifteenth Street School and how much I have learned from them and from their parents. We passed the dark monolith of the Women's House of Detention. I looked up at

118

it and then I looked past it at the sky and there they were
—the little orgones, tumbling over each other, playing
leapfrog and skipping and dancing for joy.

"Holy Christ, honey," I said, "look at them up there,
the orgones. They don't care about any of it, do they?"
Carolyn looked up at them and laughed and squeezed my
hand and we went home.

Dr. Baker has written a book called Man in the Trap *(Macmillan), which explains in casebook form the various methods of treatment in orgonomy. I recommend it to anyone who would like a further understanding of the subject.*